ONE-MAN TEAM

THE MATT LE TISSIER STORY

ONE-MAN TEAM

THE MATT LE TISSIER STORY

Lloyd Pettiford

ARDRA PRESS

First published in 2005 by
Ardra Press
PO Box 78
Cottingham
HU16 4WT
United Kingdom
www.ardrapress.com

The right of Lloyd Pettiford to be identified as the author of this work has been asserted by him in accordance with the Copyright, Designs and Patents Act 1988.

ISBN: 0-9548678-2-3

British Library Cataloguing in Publication Data
A CIP record for this book can be obtained from the British Library

Designed and typeset by Julie Martin

Printed and bound by TJ International Ltd, Padstow, Cornwall

Cover design by Ciaron Lee Marlow
www.rockers-going-starwars.co.uk

For 'Little M'
(Hope you don't mind not being called Matthew!?
This is what you missed)

Contents

Acknowledgements

These acknowledgements are written in the sure knowledge that I shall miss out someone who deserves to be put in. For which apologies in advance; there are just so many people who love Matty and have offered opinions or advice on this book. That said, definitely not included is anyone who doesn't share my total admiration; thus if you are a dear friend of mine but subscribe to the 'he was good, *but...*' school, you'll not find yourself mentioned here. So, in no particular order apart from the first one who is my wife, thanks to you all.

Norksy, Mike, Andy, Mike and all the Midlands Saints, Jamie, Stu, Band, Andy and Matt (the Black Sea Saints), Cardy (a Saints fan stuck in a Chelsea fan's body), Tom Mitchell, Paul Jarvis, Lee Robinson, Tony and the Chan brothers and anyone else who was in Bucharest, Roger and Ann Van Dyck, Karsten Hubscher (the original Bremen Saint), David Knox and some of his Werder Barman 5-a-side team, the family Whitfield and Dougal McSporran, David Humphreys, Owen, Roger Young, Alan and all the Cardiff Saints (even though I don't know them), Fred from The Family Cat and anyone else who never forgot and never lost the faith (which doesn't include the fat misogynist mutant who sat in front of us at Wimbledon that time).

Matthew Smith, I'm not sure you deserve to be in that list of adorers or not, but thanks anyway for comments, encouragement and for helping make this happen. No thanks at all for your former employer who gave me a contract but then didn't publish but many thanks to Ronan Fitzsimons and Ardra Press for enthusiastically stepping in.

As well as match programmes (including Le Tissier's testimonial) I have also consulted various websites including **www.saintsforever.com**, another one about ugly footballers that rather unjustly includes Matty and one called **www.mattletiss.com** that seems, alas, to have run out of steam. Thanks to the hard-working Pete Wilkin, who came through with an idea when Matty didn't want to play.

Matthew Le Tissier declined to be involved in this book despite the fact that I offered to give all my royalties to his favourite charity but I would, nonetheless, like to thank him for inspiring me to write such a book and providing such an interesting topic to research. I guess he gets asked to do a lot of stuff so I don't blame him. One also can't help thinking that 'advisers' or 'agents' might be behind this as he originally indicated a desire to be involved. Perhaps they feel that this book will get in the way of any Le Tissier autobiography which will appear in the future? Perhaps Matty simply couldn't be arsed? I can understand that; he's not to know that I happen to be his biggest fan!

Realising that Matty would not contribute in any way to the book was a disappointing end to a very enjoyable process, but I am not tempted to re-write the book in any negative way. Fame brings its own pressures and presumably more requests than it is possible to deal with; there is no particular reason why my request should have been favoured. It makes me sad though; getting this written in my spare time also brought plenty of pressures which I would think Matty, in his turn, would also not understand! So finally thank you to me. I hope you enjoy the book!

Finally just to mention that Matty does a lot of work for Dr

Barnados; thanks to them for trying to enlist Matty's help. In the end the royalties will go to the NSPCC, for no other reason than I wanted to give the money to a children's charity to celebrate the birth of our daughter Emma and my Mum does voluntary work for them. I think it is also worth drawing your attention to these people: Kids Company. Please check out their website and make a donation – with thanks. **www.kidsco.org.uk**

Lloyd Pettiford
Nottingham
30 January 2005

(One day after beating Pompey in the FA Cup with a dodgy 93rd minute penalty, but – alas – still adrift in the relegation zone)

Preface

Nabat Books is a series which is dedicated to reprinting the memoirs of misfits and outsiders. Whilst that particular series – connected with AK Press in the UK – is concerned with political matters, their explanatory blurb (slightly amended or interpreted for a football context) gives some insight into why Matthew Le Tissier will always be a bit more relevant than any number of Beckhams, Zidanes and Ronaldos.

To be a contemporary success they argue is 'highly toxic' – wealth, fame and power are a poison cocktail. A world obsessed with measuring success through money ('triumphal capitalism') enshrines the most dismal tendencies like greed and self-interest as the wellsprings of civilisation. Although talking about corporate conglomerates and a sickening US foreign policy amongst other things, their contention that the winners' view of history is deeply lame and soul-rotting stuff could equally be applied to Manchester United, Arsenal, Real Madrid etc.

They argue that in a world of 'crushed hopes, mountains of corpses and the commodification of everything', the interesting stories therefore lie on the margins of society. Their reprinted autobiographies of Jack Black (no, not the fat bloke in *Shallow Hal*), James Carr and François Eugène Vidocq bear testimony to this argument if you find the time to seek them out. Though it would be foolish to put footballers in this same category of 'drop-outs, dissidents, renegades and revolutionaries' it is similarly true that the interesting stories are not of those who did what they were supposed to and achieved what they should have done but those who did not.

Whether through choice, carelessness or against their will, the stories of players such as Robin Friday, Eduard Streltsov and Matthew Le Tissier will always be more interesting than David Beckham's 'side' or Alan Shearer's creosoted fence. It must not be forgotten that Matthew Le Tissier will always be special not only for what he did, but also for what he did not do (whether by choice or not). In the telling of a story, this player's almost limitless sense of promise must always be borne in mind.

Introduction:

Gets the Ball, Takes the Piss

Note: One day, Matt Le Tissier will write an autobiography. Indeed as we go to press I am told it's on its way. Doubtless it will be brilliant. But until he gets around to it, here's my take on things...

'Matt Le Tiss, Matt Le Tiss, Matt Le, Matt Le Tiss, he gets the ball, an' 'e takes the piss...Matt Le, Matt Le Tiss'. It may seem entirely appropriate that for the footballer whose relaxed genius was so misunderstood by too many so-called 'experts', even the 'Tiss-Piss' rhyme in his song is lazy. That word – lazy – haunted Le Tissier's career, boiling down the talents of a quick-witted, as well as quick-footed, player into a simple dichotomous debate: Matty was either a sublime genius who was good enough to 'take the piss' out of virtually anybody on a football field, or he was a lazy luxury, a perhaps likeable waster who could have made so much more of himself. To reduce the argument in this way is fundamentally to misunderstand however.

And let's get one thing straight from the outset: there will be no such silly debate here. For a start it is far too simplistic; for another thing, Matty was marvellous and he was fantastic. He was simply the best. A world class footballer whom England sportingly decided it would be unfair to let loose on an unsuspecting world; another triumph for our legendary sense of fair-play! A God. And for those who followed his career closely it was not just those famous and numerous goals that make the debate about his greatness completely and utterly nonsensical. It was the flicks and tricks and the vision good enough to 'play in' other players of only modest talent, all at 'struggling Southampton', and very often with the threat of relegation looming.

Those who didn't like Le Tissier rarely understood that they were not dealing with a player whose work-rate might be improved or who needed to get involved more, but a player who could actually do things that others couldn't; a *unique* talent should not – and of course can not – be compared, but just needs to be appreciated for what it is. Many of *these* people now try and look back on his career by describing him as some kind of giant Jabba the Hutt-type creature whom Saints kept in a wheelbarrow and only pushed onto the pitch to take corners, free-kicks and penalties – a gross caricature of a player who certainly prior to 1997 had no little pace.

And if he didn't track back and tackle? Well for those who have seen his efforts at tackling – comical kicking at the ankles of Eric Cantona at The Dell springs to mind – this can only be seen as an ability to recognise what you don't do well. For a player whose timing and 'eye' meant that he was as unlikely to miss the ball as he was to volunteer for extra training, it is quite extraordinary how often he kicked the opponent when supposedly aiming for the ball. Even an early 'Le Tissier for England' piece ('Magic Matt for England') in the Southampton *Daily Echo* from January 1990 conceded that 'he cannot tackle to save his life'!

So yes, Matty could have worked harder in training, watched his diet a little (or a lot) better, fitted more into a team pattern and shown a ruthless ambition to win medals. But then again he might have injured himself (his tackling being somewhat akin to Gascoigne in that cup final, if he ever indulged). On the other hand such behaviour might have meant that he also repressed the audacious flair that allowed him to let players catch up with him, just so he could take them out of the game again with a nutmeg or, what is more, he might have played for (shudder at the thought) Manchester United. So, I think Matty looks back with pride on what he achieved; surely there is no reason to do otherwise. He argues that without the freedom to enjoy it – and to do it 'his way' – he may well not have found the motivation at all. So, once in a lifetime comes a player who you simply don't want to leave your club; it wasn't Shearer, Wallace, Flowers, Kenna, Bridge or Beattie. It was Matty. And to think, we got to hold on to Franny Benali too...[1]

Matty himself says that his ambitions were to score goals in England's top division and play for England. He did both, with nearly 200 of the former (some of his 209 goals coming in cup competitions) and a mere 8 caps. But it is true that others wanted him to achieve loftier ambitions and even now base their criticisms on what *they* feel he *ought* to have done. Many said so in a way that suggested his unwillingness to move somehow made him a worse player (or person), very often one suspects because they would have had Le God in their team in an instant. As the banner in the Brazil section at the pre-Euro 1996 fixture between England and Brazil said: 'Brazil would pick Le Tiss.' Although to quote that particular banner is slightly

---

[1] At the time of writing Francis Benali has just left Southampton after 22 years' service. Phew!

cheating – because I made and displayed said banner myself. Several rows behind me another said (in Portuguese) 'Where is Le Tissier?' Indeed, that is the question! Where was he when honours were won, where was he when England missed penalties and lacked creativity, and where was he when Southampton finally got to a cup final? Is it a sad tale or a happy one? I can see why some would characterise it as a tale of 'what might have been' but as a Southampton fan, I don't think I'd change a thing, and listening to the man himself you suspect that if things were not going to happen on his terms, he'd be happy enough that they did not happen at all.

Obsession

Before moving on to look at the career of the great man/deity, it is perhaps necessary to emphasise – to allow this account to be put in perspective - that not only can there be no debate over the genius of Le Tissier, but that more than that, Matty could do no wrong (for me), or at least I could forgive him anything. When I first became really aware of him, I was sometimes changing light-bulbs in Tesco and sometimes claiming benefit (when all the bulbs had been changed obviously) and trying to finish a PhD thesis that only 3 people have ever read and are ever likely to read. My life consisted of boiling up frozen peas and putting them in oxtail soup for tea (because that was quite literally all that was left – and when I say 'quite literally' I don't mean in the way that David Pleat means it when he says 'Kevin Davies literally has no left foot'). I don't want you to feel too sorry for me, although it is true that most of my money (as if I was some kind of modern day George Orwell *Down and Out in Stoke and Southampton!*) was spent on Mother's Pride, Stork SB and Romanian Pinot Noir (which weighed in at an impressive, duty-busting £1.79 – they were literally giving it away). Pilchards were a luxury; a visit to the launderette a rarity..

However, my temporary registration as a student ('writing up') also allowed me a free flat (as a warden), an overdraft facility (thanks to the infinitely patient and rather lovely Mrs Price of Midland Bank), access to squash courts and a social life. Looking back, life was actually a pretty easy round of red wine, student parties, nurses and squash; but at the time it suited my self-pitying persona to regard it as utterly miserable in the style of *Withnail and I*. It seemed like I would never get a PhD and that I was destined for life on the scrap-heap. And then someone – a steward (friend of a friend) – started to get me into The Dell for free for games that weren't sold out (which they used to have way back in 1993/94).

All of a sudden, at least every other Saturday or so, I knew

I was going to see something that even a childhood of supporting the mighty Bishop's Stortford FC had not prepared me for.[2] Something amazing and magical; a world class player in my town! Even on the radio I was spell-bound. By the end of Norwich City 4-5 Southampton, a game in which Matty scored a hat-trick and Saints led for just 1 minute at the end, I suddenly realised at 4.55 that the bath I was lying in had gone stone cold, so transfixed had I become by the 'back to Carrow Roads' which interrupted the commentary game that day. As an important aside it is worth noting that the own goal scored by Robert Ullathorne in that game was just about the only Saints goal between Christmas and the end of the season (1993/94) that Le Tissier did not either score himself or provide the assist for!

When I got married I wanted us both to change our names to Le Tissier. My wife preferred the feminist statement of the woman not changing her name but I wanted to go further. I was serious. I then drunkenly argued with my new wife over her assertion that she would not be unfaithful to me if MLT offered his services or demanded hers – I argued that this was something she ought to be prepared to do if required. I was serious. In my career as it developed (I was not on a self-pitying scrap-heap after all) I have seemingly

[2] Although Karl 'the weasel' Zacchau had his moments, mind you.

forgotten the kindness and help of others and dedicated the academic books I have written to Le Tissier (although in the case of the PhD – it should be said – he did get *joint* billing along with various family and friends, as well as Romanian Pinot Noir and several student nurses). I became obsessed. I am obsessed. Our spare room is a shrine full of signed shirts, photos and those silly little plastic models that were popular for a while and make a comeback of sorts every now and again. The one in an England kit is almost too painful to behold.

Writing this book then is part of my obsession and I ask you to forgive its partiality; I for one think the allegedly balanced media version and the opinions of Terry Vegetables need to be seriously redressed. Venables once said (after a teletext poll revealed 83% thought Terry was wrong not to have picked Matty for England) that 'people want him to play, he wants to play and I want him to play' but it seems he probably did mean it in *that* specific order. But whilst this book is, of course, a labour of love and may therefore be ever so slightly biased on occasion, if you disagree with my assessment you can at least be reassured that some of your pennies will find their way to charity and in particular to the NSPCC.

So, here you have my best efforts to describe not just the genius of the man, but also to give a sense of the pain of those who genuinely think that the 1990s could have been so much different for the English national team with his help. Where I can, I shall stick to the facts of the matter, but where you need to know, I'll be telling you the truth. This is a player who has been seriously misunderstood – even if he sometimes appeared his own worst enemy – and those (at least) who watched him week in and week out *will* understand.

The Order

Beginning at the beginning, the opening chapter covers Matty's childhood. If Francis Benali, known as the 'divine hoof' in our house, could play centre-forward for England U16 and dance through defences at school level, you'd expect that Le Tiss would have been totally lethal in his days of 'small boys in the park, jumpers for goalposts', and indeed in his last season on Guernsey he knocked in 169 goals. However, even then there is some evidence that his class mates would have to toil around after the ball for 89 minutes (while Matty 'created space' for himself) and hope that sooner or later young Matty would shake off his lethargy and knock one in from a corner or dribble round the opposition. Indeed Le Tissier's PE teacher, John Henry, recalls several occasions when the yawning wunderkind actually had to be reminded to score; upon which he would waltz around 6 players and score. He was also very good at cricket, although rarely known to scream for the quick single.

The second chapter is titled 'The Thin Years'; indeed in video footage of Le Tissier's early career, it is quite difficult to recognise the gangly youth on the far touchline making his Saints debut. One can only assume that the McDonald's franchise arrived late on Guernsey and that 'the kebab' is an alien concept, although come to think of it, since I have never been to Guernsey they may still be lucky enough to have avoided said gastronomic delights. But in any case, it is extraordinary to think how skinny was the lad who made his debut for Southampton age 17. Indeed, his very frailty was probably a reason why, despite his extraordinary skill, he didn't 'do a Rooney' and become an instant hit or fixture in the team. Ultimately, some may feel him to have overdone it a bit when told to 'bulk up a bit, lad' but most people I have ever heard complaining about his weight were doing so whilst tucking into a glass of beer and plate of chips.

We then come to the Branfoot Years. If one were to subscribe to the 'playing for Southampton cost Le Tissier an England career' thesis, then surely it was during these years that this most applied, as Le Tissier's talents were 'shown off' for a team encouraged to 'clog' their way to victory by a manager with neither the intellect nor the ability to work out what to do with a world class talent. If Le Tiss had been properly show-cased and encouraged in these years (which were, even so, quite successful) then perhaps an early England debut might have changed the whole story? But, what a football genius was Ian Branfoot! In 1993/94 he dropped Le Tissier for five games during which the Saints failed to win. Indeed at one point, Saints failed to win for over 20 games, over a number of seasons, in matches where Le Tiss had been dropped, injured or suspended. Branfoot then recalled Matty for a televised game against Newcastle. The game is most often remembered for Le Tissier scoring two sublime goals which finished first and third in Sky's goal of the season competition. Southampton, who created little else that day, or indeed *ever* under Branfoot, won 2-1 and eventually scraped enough points to survive in the Premiership once Branfoot had been shown the door in the nick of time.

It is worth pointing out that if Andy Cole had taken more than 1 of his open goals the 2-10 scoreline might have been remembered as much as Le Tiss's goals. It is also worth pointing out that as Le Tissier flicked the ball with the back of his heel, over two defenders and then calmly into the back of the net, Branfoot was preparing to substitute him with a player with all the grace of a giraffe – name of

Paul Moody. Still, afterwards, Branfoot was happy to claim all the credit.

Le Tissier's goals probably kept Mr Branfoot in his job longer than the ungrateful 'football genius' deserved. In terms of keeping his job, Le Tissier probably did the same for Alan Ball. But at least Bally recognised what he had and got the best out of Matty. And when you look at Alan Ball's record it really isn't terribly good and he never got anywhere near that same level of success with any other of his players! But Bally loved Le Tiss; Matty was *his* genius. In training, the other players were assembled around Matt and told that their job was to give him the ball. Le Tissier was made captain. He responded with a perfect swinging corner onto the head of Neil Maddison and a goal to win away at Newcastle (a 25-yard free-kick to complete a season's hat-trick of horror for the hapless Hooper in the Newcastle goal) and a hat-trick at home to Liverpool on St Valentine's day. Le Tissier's genius was evident week in week out as Saints became a one-man team. Over the season's closing weeks, 2 assists and a goal in beating Blackburn 3-1, 2 assists and 2 goals in beating Villa 4-1 combined with 2 goals and a mesmerising assist in gaining an all important 3-3 draw at West Ham on the final day meant that despite Branfoot's best efforts, the Saints survived again.

At the end of the following season, ostensibly more comfortable for the Saints, Le Tissier kept Southampton in the Premiership again. Despite starting well and ultimately finishing ninth, they had spent much of the season drifting towards the bottom of the table on the back of too many draws, and it was with not very many games left that Saints were finally mathematically safe after a 3-1 home win against Crystal Palace. Alan Smith – then Palace manager – summed it up: 'The difference between the teams was 3 words – Matthew Le Tissier...it was a case of Le Tissier versus Crystal Palace.'

Eventually, Le Tissier's sensational form under Alan Ball led to louder and louder calls for his inclusion in the England squad, especially after Graham Taylor (international football's Mr Branfoot) failed to lead Eng-er-land to USA 1994. To look at the goals Le Tissier scored for Southampton in the period 1994-96 is to be bewildered that he never did so for England and was never given more chance to. Occasionally, after picking up a few caps Matty would respond to the chant 'You'll Never Play for England' by indicating with his fingers that he *had* played for England. But sadly he always had enough fingers to do this, even without his thumbs. Those who sang the song, or the more offensive 'he's got a f****** big nose', were often rewarded with a goal and quite possibly wondered themselves if he might not be the missing piece in the England jigsaw. But it seems it was never meant to be; even the games he played were full of 'oh so nears', from the crisp but rising half-volleyed shot in his debut substitute appearance v Denmark, to the rare inaccurate free-kick in the match abandoned v Eire and the flick and agonisingly close volley with his 'wrong' foot v Romania.

But it is probably the World Cup qualifying game against Italy that still causes most debate. A vital, early game under new England manager Glenn Hoddle and a real chance for Matty to shine on the biggest stage. But Le Tissier's brother had blurted to the press that Hoddle was going to play Matty. It was a bad omen. It felt wrong. Tense, I drank 8 pints in no time and a fight went off in another part of the pub I was in. Like the Eire abandonment it just felt like it would never happen...and it didn't. Nice flicks, blocked shots, headers just wide...Le Tissier was to blame according to the press, even though Hoddle admitted he was wrong (unusual) in taking him off just at the time when he had been doing the most damage in the Premiership, as defences tire in the latter stages. Perhaps, left on, Le Tissier – who actually played pretty well if you go back to the video – might have unlocked the tight Italian defence, but we shall never know. The game became Le Tissier's crucifixion as the press looked for someone to blame. Hoddle was happy to join in, as Matty never played for England again.

I heard the Italy game described as Le Tissier's 'crucifixion' in a pub in Shepherd's Bush just before he appeared to be getting a chance to prove himself again with selection for England B v Russia B. Bloody hell, it seemed that everyone there was a Le Tiss nut like me. We all wanted to believe that this would be the resurrection. Le Tiss had just been *too* good to keep on ignoring and so Hoddle gave him his 'chance' against Russia B at Loftus Road. To start with it didn't look good. He was dispossessed in midfield and a shot hit the post. But by the end he'd scored 3 well-taken goals and gone close several more times before going off to a hero's reception and with the captain's armband via Ferdinand and Anderton. 'Hod, please pick Le God' read the most quoted banner following the 4-1 success. Then, on the last day of the season, Le Tissier scored Saints' goal in a 1-1 draw against Spurs at White Hart Lane with Hoddle in attendance. 'Matty's goin' t'France' sang the crowd.

But he didn't. He didn't even make the team that drew 0-0 with the might of Saudi Arabia in the next warm-up game for the full side. Though Hoddle had once described Le Tissier as England's most creative player, once he became England manager he treated him much more shoddily than he himself had been treated when deserving of that description. (As I write, Southampton have just beaten Spurs 1-3 at White Hart Lane – their first victory there since Le Tissier's brace clinched a 1-2 victory in 1994/95. The crowd – many of the same people who sang 'Matty's goin' t'France' one suspects – sang rousing choruses of 'Now you've gotta believe us, you're gonna get the sack' to Glenn Hoddle. And he was. The next day. At least Hoddle's dreams have always been killed by his own choice of words and the weakness of his *own* performance; and perhaps his warped ideas of karma and divine retribution have something in them after all?)

Le Tissier never seemed to recover from that rejection. True, there was the occasional spark of genius, but then again you'd expect that from, err, well, a genius. But anyone who's struggling to get in a side ahead of Uwe Rosler was clearly in decline. And what a sharp decline it was. We would all hope, each and every time, that another comeback was just around the corner. He remained a total hero, however ineffectual. But niggling injury followed niggling injury and Le Tissier, who had always got fit by playing, was piling on the pounds. He did, at least, score the final goal at The Dell and played – his loyalty having earned an extra year's contract – at the new St Mary's stadium, the dream of which his skills had almost single-handedly kept alive in the days before Pahars and Beattie. His testimonial was a giant act of worship.

Despite the fact that opposing supporters ditched 'you'll never play for England' and replaced it with Reebok's 'belly's gonna get ya!', off the field, life for Le Tiss had certainly got interesting. Unable to get into the team he turned up and sat with the supporters at various games with different women on his arm. (John Beresford's comment in the Le Tiss testimonial magazine is intriguing: 'Don't go chatting up any birds where there's a boyfriend with a bottle in his hand!') At Coventry one such 'bird' (I do apologise for having to report such derogatory, sexist terms) was subjected to so much abuse that they had to leave; the reasons were unclear – perhaps a friend of Matty's recently dumped childhood sweetheart, wife and mother of his children? At Liverpool he was accompanied by Emily Symons (Marylin out of *Home and Away* and now of *Emmerdale* fame). In fact it was probably because of her connection that long after Le Tiss had ceased to play for England he nevertheless played for The World (against Australia). Le Tissier was still grabbing the headlines, but his career was clearly coming to an end.

The exception to the rule of decline was, of course, the fairytale finish at The Dell. Though unable to guarantee even a place on the bench by this point, both Le Tissier and Benali were brought on for a few minutes at the end to take the applause of the crowd. However, the atmosphere was electric – I know because I had to sit on a wall outside with a radio to 'be a part of it' – and the crowd expected something to happen. With the score at 2-2 a dubious penalty appeal was turned down; the crowd bayed their clear disapproval, knowing that a penalty would be taken by Matty and almost certainly result in a goal. However, a penalty would not have been remembered the same way as a trademark control, swivel and beautifully balanced half-volley into the top corner to win the match in the 89th minute...with his 'wrong' foot.

After all the 'oh so nears' it was the right way to 'end' Le Tissier's career, adding just one more fantastic memory. Though this book finishes by reflecting upon his occasional experiences at St Mary's, then in beach soccer, Masters football and at Eastleigh, ultimately there is no other conclusion to draw than that Matthew Le Tissier was the finest English footballer of his generation, and whilst people may suggest that *he* missed out career-wise, in reality it was *England* that missed out. We all missed out. Matty on the other hand has had a very nice life, thank you. Matty is a legend.

At the start of the 'Unbelievable' video, David Baddiel suggests that 'Matthew Le Tissier is worshipped on the south coast – hardly surprising when every season he single-handedly saves Southampton from relegation.' It is a shoddy dialogue which suggests that this fact would make him popular all along the 'south coast', and for Pompey fans it must have been particularly frustrating as they hung on to their own divisional status each year just to find out that Saints weren't joining them in Division One after all. But the fact is that Le Tissier's goals and inspiration *were* enough – just – to keep Saints in the top flight season after season. Their new stadium, cup final appearance and on-going Premiership status really *are* all due to him. How many times did opposing fans claim that he did nothing all game – *except* score the winner (and keep 2 or 3 defenders permanently occupied of course)? So whilst others may claim the title – most notably Maradona for Argentina in 1990 – does anyone else really deserve the accolade 'one-man team' as much as Matthew Le Tissier? It is one 'modest (though confident) Matt' would probably reject for himself, but when you think of the players he has played alongside – Heaney, Benali, Dowie and various 'stars' past their best – it is surely one he deserves. You'd have to be from another planet not to think Matty was the best; although the existence of 'Matty for England' crop circles suggests that maybe even 'they' know the truth out there...

Chapter 1:

The Early Years

Disclaimer – Please skip this chapter if scandal is what you're after. Whilst childhood can seem terribly important at the time, it isn't always. In terms of entertainment value, Matt Le Tiss did not have alcoholic parents, famous parents, or abusive parents. He was not gifted enough to have gone to Oxford University as an 8-year-old, nor did he fall in with the wrong crowd when he was 13 and sniff glue. No, he lived on Guernsey, played sport with his older brothers who no doubt roughed him up or defended him depending on their age, and dreamed of being a professional footballer. For birds and booze, please see later chapters.

In the Beginning: Childhood According to Saint Matthew

Born on 14 October 1968 in St Peter Port, Guernsey, Matthew Le Tissier grew up to be just over 6 foot tall (I think that's about 1 metre 85 cm). Weight-wise it is difficult to be so precise as he seems, rather like yours truly, to be one of those people whose weight changes regularly, usually in an upward direction and occasionally downwards as training and half-hearted dieting have fleeting effects. I just don't think naturally skinny people realise how hard it is, although also like yours truly a liking for lager-type drinks (OK, most kinds of drinks) and a dislike for salad do not always appear to have helped the Le Tissier cause weight-wise. That may seem like a strange start to a chapter on childhood, but with such a normal childhood this is going to take some padding I can tell you; go on, skip to the next chapter if you want ... anyway, back to Guernsey.

Matthew Paul God Le Tissier was the fourth and final son in the family, having 3 older brothers, Mark, Kevin and Carl. Though Le Tissier modestly recalls (or is it bigheadedly in a nice way?) that he didn't spend hours working on the game but just found he could naturally do things with a football that others couldn't, Ruth and Marcus – his parents – recall that he did indeed spend an awful lot of time playing football, regularly nut-megging his mother and the occasional, occasional table before knocking ornaments off the mantelpiece with crisp half-volleys, when he should have been helping out in preparing dinner by shelling peas (which he apparently found more difficult).

His natural talent also saw him excel at cricket, tennis, golf, softball and almost everything except – as David Baddiel trying to be funny says – 'haircuts'; when asked what he would change if he were 17 again, Le Tiss answered 'my haircut', so Baddiel may have a point. Looking at early pictures of our hero he might also have included 'jumpers', but that was, in fairness, something about the time more than the man.

Anyway, young Le Tissier was confident, finding that he just seemed to know what to do with the ball, and (much!) more importantly, that he could actually do it (I mean we all score with those 25-yard volleys in our dreams). This confidence – which even he says at that age might have been construed as big-headedness – is probably an important reason why he was able to leave Guernsey, unlike his brothers who, though all talented footballers, preferred to stay on the island. Self-confidence is also why he was able to survive a career as one of the best and most underrated players in the world at a club that normally struggles to attract world-class players even when they are claiming old age pensions – for example Oliver Beerhoof.[3] (At the time of writing, a Cup Final appearance and wins against Manchester United must surely suggest a disturbance in the force).[4]

In the magazine accompanying his testimonial, Le Tissier begins by saying that when he was seven years old and growing up in Guernsey, he dreamed of being a professional footballer and playing for England. He rightly points out that this is no different from any other kid. But there is a big difference between dream and reality and that isn't just like any other kid. My own sworn intent to run a marathon and become Communist prime minister and share sweets (that being my 7-year-old 'vision' of 'democratic socialism' in action) missed the mark somewhat of my pot-bellied, physically slothful and politically apathetic self. Le Tissier goes

[3] Oliver Bierhoff was a big bustling German centre-forward. Probably no better or worse than Iain Dowie, he nonetheless suggested – as a 33-year-old – that a club like Southampton were not really in his league. What this really meant was that a club like Southampton couldn't be so profligate with their money that they could throw it at players who were seeing out their careers; not since Branfoot had tried that approach in the Speedie/Dixon days.

[4] Alas, in revising the manuscript, the bad old days appear to have returned with Southampton already locked in a grim relegation struggle before Christmas.

on to claim, however, that 'even at that young age I knew I was going to do it. I knew I had been blessed with natural ability and that was what I was born to do.' Fair enough, and this self-belief has certainly helped Matty and allowed him to shrug off the boo-boys (*always* the other team's fans, it must be said) but I have talked to a 10-year-old boy with a Big Mac in his mouth, another in his hand and another in a bag waiting to be eaten who, despite being taller lying on his back than standing up, was still convinced he was the next Bobby Charlton. However much Matty is able to take for granted his exceptional talent, we should not assume this remarkable story was, in fact, inevitable.

Le Tissier's talent, especially as a footballer, meant that he was regularly playing in older age groupings. He had made the school under 11 team by the time he was 8 and scored a couple of goals to win his first medal. This is remarkable when you consider that boys like David Cogan (you know the one, singed his hair with a bunsen burner?) were completely grey and shaving twice a day by the time they were 11. Dwarfed in the team shot, Matty has always managed to stand out for one reason or another (alas including the jumpers), although he had to cope with the doubters even then who suggested that however good he might be kicking around with the Guernsey lads, he wouldn't be able to make the jump to the mainland stage.

Even at this young age, his trademark loyalty (or is it – yawn – lack of ambition?) shone through. Having passed exams for the Grammar School he persuaded his parents to send him to the school about a minute from his front door instead. Was this simply laziness? Was it loyalty to his friends? Or was it the first statement of an emerging and astute politically conscious mind; a radical political statement ('propaganda by deed' if you like) about elitism in higher education and part of a lifelong crusade, epitomised by his loyalty to Saints, to stand on the side of fairness and justice against oppressive bourgeois society and privilege? He says he just wanted to be with his friends. But those who would see this as early evidence of lack of ambition should reflect a moment and be ashamed of themselves. Should 'career success' or 'ambition' really be defined in terms of wanting more money and things (i.e. avarice and greed) or wanting honours showered upon you to prove your worth (i.e. the sin of pride), or is it OK for your ambition in life simply to be happy? Not a sin is it? With apologies for the heartfelt interlude, it is the *world* which is out of step on the question of ambition!

Having elected to stay with his friends, senior school saw Matty attract more and more attention as he became physically stronger. His PE teacher John Henry claimed that he didn't teach the young Matty much, which just goes to show what you get from a Comprehensive School education these days. Although what I think he meant was that having first seen Matty knocking in goals direct from a corner as an 8-year-old, he realised that the boy didn't really need much technical coaching, certainly not from a PE teacher, although I dare say Mr Henry was nicer than the bald and moustachioed (respectively) pillocks who passed for mine. Like with many subsequent managers, Henry talks – half smile, half regret – about Matt's lackadaisical days and of needing to remind him of the score before he would then waltz around 6 players to knock in winning goals. Even then, he was a one-man team; even then it was a question of what more it might be possible to get from him.

Guernsey

According to my extensive research and vivid imagination, Guernsey's geographical location provides a perfect climate for kids to get outside and practise football. Meanwhile the historical closeness to France and wartime invasion by Germany have led to a confidence more commonly associated with the modern European foreigner than your 'umble Brit. Add to this the tax-haven status which has seen money flood in to fund a prosperous economy able to support an army of 'monkey butlers' to cater for people's every need, and you have the perfect combination for kids to grow up laid-back and confident.

Egg, Chips and Creosote

So, in his last season on Guernsey Matt lethargically dragged his way around the pitch to knock in 169 goals. No doubt the Guernsey equivalent of Jimmy Hill – or whichever pundit – feels that had he applied himself he could have scored 300. Or that 169 *was* a pretty good total but that his overall contribution to the team just wasn't enough. But anyway, after an unhappy trial at Oxford (now I'd like to have seen him stay with Oxford for 17 years to prove his loyalty!) he moved to Southampton as an apprentice in 1985 and found a nice family to provide him with a home from home. Pete Ford (a season ticket holder) and Pat (his wife) took young Matt into their home, quite possibly scarring their own children for life by forcing them to share a room as a result of the new arrival. Already the young Matthew was demonstrating an unerring ability to make space for himself.

Although Pete Ford recalls that Matt was a 'real skinny lad', he also recalls that he rejected the lovely salad that had been provided for him – and they say that it is only *now* that professional footballers are spoiled – and insisted instead on egg and chips. Rumours that this 'veggie filth' then drove him to his regrettable kebab and quarter-pounder addiction are unsubstantiated, but it *does* appear that this family atmosphere helped Matt settle in away from home. I have not yet made my pilgrimage to Guernsey, but I hear it's lovely. On the other hand I have lived in Southampton and it must have been a shock, so I guess Saints fans should be grateful that Pete and Pat didn't take a more 'you'll eat what you are given when you're under our roof' type of line.

On whatever 'fatty fuel', Matty went on to score over 50 goals in a season for the youth team, including 6 in one game versus Brighton. Dave Merrington – his manager at the time – admitted that young Le Tiss was sometimes lazy but added that he also had a touch of genius. Indeed, although all footballers might have weaknesses, Merrington was able to see that one needed to see beyond any frustration with what Matty couldn't do, because there was so much he could do that others couldn't. As Mick Channon pointed out, most brilliant footballers have similarities with other brilliant footballers, whereas Le Tiss was just unique; Merrington was able to see this and Matty was even able to repay him. Years later, for Merrington's one season in charge at The Dell, that genius shone just enough to keep Saints in the Premiership again, although not enough to keep Merrington his job...more on that story later. Matty also gave Dave the shirt from his first international appearance.

What Didn't Happen Next

The fact that Matty picked up a few international appearances, during which he was never given a proper run but still conjured up enough moments of magic for those who were looking, makes the question of what might have happened even more painful. But if Matty had been thrown in earlier, even though his physique meant he could never have done a Rooney, what might have happened? In 1994, the worst that might have happened was the same as what actually happened. And when one thinks of the squad players who were never used, wouldn't it have been better to have had Le Tiss on the bench? And when we needed penalty takers? The fact that Le Tiss plays wicket-keeper and does a tolerable goal-keeping impression in warm-ups might have justified his selection in the untried '3rd goalie/genius' position. Anything but the total waste would have been preferable. 1990, 1992, 1994, 1996 and 1998 could have been so different. They might not have been, I'll grant you, but as Simon Barnes (quoted more fully in Chapter 4) argues: 'no other player conveys that sense of almost limitless possibility.' That's it in essence – it is not that we *would* have done better with Le Tiss but that we quite clearly could have. Perhaps the 1990 World Cup was too soon, but in Paul Gascoigne it showed what might be done if England trusted in flair. 1992 and 1994 could not have been any worse with Le Tiss playing, now could they? 1996 and 1998 were OK but not only is the semi-finals at home in a major Championship of 16 teams only around par for the course, but we lost on penalties and in 1998 did so again – all this after Le Tiss didn't even get the chance to prove himself in a Wembley bore draw versus the mighty Saudis. So it would be pointless to argue that X and Y would definitely have happened if Le Tiss had been given a proper international run. No one knows. But everyone knows that something much better *could* have happened. By taking the same old conservative England route we will never know what sublime pleasure we might have experienced, only that the best player of a generation looked on as we won f*** all.

In Le Tissier's testimonial magazine, Merrington recalls his first glimpse of genius. 'He was 17 years old and the youth team were playing away at Oxford. The score at half-time was 0-0 and Matthew was told to free himself and roam anywhere across the front line. Within five minutes of the second half he received a ball with his back to play on the halfway line. Closely marked by an opponent he casually flicked the ball over his head, and went directly for goal, side-stepping the next defender with a body swerve. He looked up, assessed the situation and calmly bent the ball around another defender and the goalkeeper. It was a fantastic goal of sheer brilliance, which would have graced any ground in the world. Needless to say, I came back and informed the then manager Chris Nicholl that in my opinion we had a sheer genius on our hands.'

As well as the goals, Matty recalls the work of an apprentice: hoovering, dusting, cleaning toilets and creosoting. Matt doesn't appear to have got the same pleasure from creosoting as Alan Shearer and I dare say failed to do it with the same determination and gusto. I'd certainly have Shearer creosoting *my* fence ahead of Le Tissier any day of the week. But Matty reserves his fondest memories for shining Joe Jordan's boots, although given the trademark aggression of the 'well respected'[5] Scottish international, it is something you would have wanted to get right. A little over a year after his arrival from Guernsey and a season in the youth team, and following just a few appearances in the reserves, Matty became a regular in the first team squad.

I Believe

Matthew Le Tissier always demonstrated great confidence in his own abilities, from a very young age and even at times when fools failed to notice or utilise them. Even so, Le Tiss has also been quite modest about what he does, partly because it has come easily and required no special effort. At the same time he has been quite gentle in his criticism of others. So what has he said, when and about whom?

'I missed a penalty in my first ever youth team game. Not a lot of people know that.' (Impression of Michael Caine from Interview in Testimonial Magazine)

---

[5] Until he moved to Pompey at least!

'Although there has been speculation that I'm going to join a so-called "bigger" club, I don't see any reason why I should change [everything] for the sake of a few quid.' (March 1995, in *Match*)

'I enjoy being a big fish in a small pond.' (In the Testimonial Magazine – small pond? Southampton? Must be getting confused with Portsmouth? Oh I see, he didn't mean it literally? I just thought what with his 'looks' and everything he was being mockingly self-ironic or something.)

'I spoke to Tim Flowers before the game and he told me that Alan Shearer's strike against QPR just 2 weeks before would win goal of the season so I shouldn't bother. That was inspiration.' Matty talks about his goal of the season 1994/95 v Blackburn (away). *Match*, 11 December 1999.

'I actually enjoy a relegation fight. I think it keeps me sharp. That may not happen if I was playing for a mid-table team.' Matthew amazingly justifies many a tortuous afternoon in the mid-1990s in *The Guardian*, August 1998.

'I was a luxury and always have been considered a luxury by most of my managers. But at some point or another they've said, "Please come back and score some goals – so I can keep my job!"' (Interview in Testimonial Magazine.)

On Venables '...he dropped me when I was playing the best football of my life ... I was 25 or 26 ... That was the best part of my career and he still didn't pick me ... that was more disappointing than being dropped by Glenn, 'cos I wasn't playing as well when Glenn was manager as I was when Terry was in charge.' (Interview in Testimonial Magazine.)

'I suppose I have been stubborn. I have wanted to win caps at Southampton to prove you don't have to move to a big club. I always thought that was wrong.' *The Guardian*, August 1998.

'I will challenge any player to play 540 games for a team that fought relegation for 12 years and score 207 goals.' Coming to the end of his career, Le Tissier answers the question as to why he should still be regarded as a great player, even in the absence of championships, European nights etc. And so he should, of course

Chapter 2:

The Thin Years

In his Saints debut (2 September 1986) against a
Tottenham Hotspur team which included Glenn Hoddle, a
fierce pass (or was it goal kick?) arrowed its way across the
pitch at about arse height. Le Tissier took the ball out of
the air and saw it land at his feet. It looked so very easy
that he really could have been trapping the proverbial 'bag
of cement' which many fans commented always seemed to
elude the likes of Carlton 'bless him but does he really have
a clue?' Palmer. He (Le Tiss) then rolled it (the ball as easy
to control as a bag of cement) through inch-perfectly – as if
to prove that it was not in fact a bag of cement – to Danny
Wallace. It all looked so easy. It also looked easier to score
than do what Wallace then did.

The words 'easy' and 'effortless' might, of course, be used

interchangeably. Effortless might, in turn, be taken literally to mean lacking in effort, and lacking in effort might, via an easy jump of logic, be compared to lazy. Right from the start, this easy (lazy?) journey from easy to lazy has been made by lazy journalists, but right from the start, it should be noted, Matt made football *look* easy. His style may not have been all bluster, but then Matty (rather than Batty) played the *beautiful* game. (Who, incidentally, would *you* rather took a penalty in a world cup eliminator?)

I have never really subscribed to the 'Le Tissier is lazy' school. I prefer to believe that good players can actually create space by not moving. Indeed, so scared of Matty were opponents, and so unable to read his flicks and tricks, that once he had the ball he was frequently able to create yards of space in an instant, not by running into it, but by merely dipping his shoulders or lifting a boot and watching others run away from him in fear of what he might produce. Besides, what is lazy? We all know people who spend hours in the office, or wherever, achieving very little…surely it is more reasonable to judge on results than simply on physical effort or time expended?

But anyway, let us just suppose for a second that there was any truth in the lazy rumour, ridiculous though it is. I have always thought this is a bit like the old joke about the dog in Le Tissier's case; the joke being 'Why does a dog lick his balls?' with the answer being 'Because he can.' In effect I am arguing 'Why was Le Tissier lazy?' Answer: 'Because he could be.' For example, St Valentine's Day, 1994, just after Alan Ball had taken over as Southampton manager from Ian Branfoot (more on that story later). Saints were cruising at The Dell against Liverpool and Matty had already knocked in 3 goals. The first goal after 23 seconds was a frighteningly fierce 25-yard half-volley which brutally silenced the travelling fans whose song tailed off in disbelief...LI-VER-POOL!, LI-VER-POOL!, LI-ver...poo....

As the snow began to arrive in occasional flecks Andy Gray opined to Sky viewers that we could 'safely say Liverpool got caught cold this evening.' He was right – one of the rare occasions I have refused a ticket in order to stay in the warm and listen to Gray's comments, however much better they are than the frighteningly low average for football commentators. The second for Matty was a penalty. Unerring as ever, although perhaps nearer to a miss than usual, it put the Saints 3-0 up after Saints' second was scored by the one and only Craig Maskell (whoooo?) from a – yawn, it's so obvious – Le Tissier corner. As for the penalty, the Liverpool fan standing by the post raised his arms to celebrate the ball sailing past the angle of post and bar only to fling them down again in frustration as the ball curved beautifully – and late – into the top corner. Le Tissier later admitted that it was further away from where he aimed than most of his penalties. But Andy Gray was right again – 'two goalkeepers couldn't have stopped it' – but like the Liverpool fan, I really thought it had missed. The third was also a penalty, perhaps overly cautious in the light of the first, but firmly enough struck to the same side to leave Brucie Grobelaar scrabbling around in the thin snow.

And so, with the game won, Le Tissier broke free. He was clean through for his 4th. But rather than running through and slotting home he aimed for the top corner from 25 yards instead. Why? Was this lazy? As the 'timber' arrived from 1997/98ish, it is tempting to think so, as we remember with sadness what Matty became unable to do which once he had achieved with ease (note 'ease'). On this occasion, Grobelaar managed to salvage pride with a fingertip save. But even the young, thin Le Tissier did this kind of thing; not, I suspect, from laziness but simply because he could. Why move to create space if you can control the ball and create space where there is none? Why run 60 yards if you can pass it to the millimetre? And why run 25 yards if you can shoot it and more or less hit the top corner each and every time? Right from the start of his career Le Tissier appeared lazy – and like in many of us there may have been times when he lacked focus or drive – but at least in part this was because when something looks *so* easy it is described as 'effortless'. And right from the start Matty made things look 'effortless'. Equals no effort. Equals (for lazy journos and stupid pundits) 'lazy'.

Anyway, after not even a handful of games for the reserves Matty was promoted to the first team, and, following a substitute appearance v Norwich, made his full debut in that midweek fixture on 2 September 1986 mentioned above. It is almost painful in historical context to hear him talk with pride of his debut being particularly special because it was against Spurs and Glenn Hoddle since Le Tissier was to become more a victim of the 'talented player' syndrome than Hoddle ever was himself. (Le Tissier also became victim of the 'love me, love my Eileen' syndrome – more on that story later.) Anyway, half of Guernsey turned up for the match apparently, having caught planes, ferries and unsafe barrels as if strapped together by desperate refugees in an effort to get there. In commentary, Tony Gubba called him Le Tee-see-ay, and interjected his commentary in surprised tone to note 'good control again from the youngster' – not something which was to surprise too many people for too long.

Snoring

In Matt's testimonial programme Timmy Flowers notes that shortly after Matt's elevation to the first team 'he achieved the pinnacle of his career, rooming with me!' Flowers goes on to note that he had to dispense with Matthew's room-sharing services due to the high volume of snoring. A later roommate, Matthew Oakley, attributes the snoring, however, to Le Tissier's advancing years. Which leaves us, of course, with an intriguing question: why don't highly paid footballers get their own room?

From then to the end of the season Le Tissier's appearances were occasional. He scored 2 goals against Manchester United in November, helping 'Big Ron' get the sack, but even that was on as a 'less than 15 minutes' substitute for Danny Wallace. In that game Le Tiss scored what he still regards as one of his best...one of those mentioned above...a cunning lob from distance rather than risking losing the ball running it towards goal. A 'lazy' lob in other words, but also brilliant. He also popped in a hat-trick against Leicester on an uncharacteristically snowy day in Southampton; for the final one dribbling round most of the Leicester team (twice) – on snow and mud.

But despite the prodigious talent, it was not a Rooney-esque rise; by the end of March local TV commentators were still opting for the slightly posh sounding Le Tee-see-ay as their preferred pronunciation. Le Tissier himself, meanwhile, was frustrated by his lack of opportunities;

Chris Nicholl said, although only later, that he was protecting Matt. Le Tiss wished he had been told, but in truth he still did not really look to have the strength to push aside defenders, even though Nicholl's strategy of protection frustrated him nonetheless.

Despite the protection from management when off the field, and the lack of physical presence when on it, Le Tissier still banged in 10 goals in that first season and Saints fans began to demand his appearance on a regular basis. It was then something of a shock to the young stripling when the following season saw only limited appearances and frequent bench-warming duties as well as complete afternoons off. Le Tissier scored only a couple of goals including his first in the FA Cup, away to Reading. A 'thin year' indeed.

However, the following season Matt did get a regular place in the side, getting into double figures and creating as many again for fellow promising youngster Rodney Wallace. Southampton were even second in the table in November during that year, although 20 games without a win and just a single point was a run which failed to maintain a Championship challenge, surprisingly enough. You don't win anything with youngsters, except when you do, as Alan Hansen has convincingly argued.

Jumper

Say 'jumper' to Matt and he might defensively say, 'jumper? I never even met 'er,' but he is more likely to say defensively, 'Ah leave it off, it was the 80s.' Look at the www.saintsforever.com tribute to Matt's account of the 1988/89 season to see one of the most hideous woollen garments ever to adorn the human form. Another Matt – this time from my 5-a-side team Werder Barman – had a school visit from a sweater-clad Le Tissier during this time and he is still in therapy

In 1989/90 Southampton managed to finish 7th and Matty became the regular number 7 – which he was to retain until the club thought that rather than respectfully retire the number it would be more fitting to give it to Andrei Kanchelskis (no comment). Anyway, 7th! – heights that the Saints took almost 15 years even to begin to approach again, with Matty's 24 league and cup goals matched again by Rod Wallace, although not by Shearer's 8 (eight). It was towards the end of this season that Le Tissier had the chance to move to Spurs. Although many Saints fans still shudder at the thought, it is a chance that Matty decided to accept...

Ugly?

As much as by his alleged laziness, Matt's early career was blighted by jumpers and haircuts that did nothing to augment his looks. Opposing fans, realising the futility of shouting 'you're lazy' at someone who's banging goals past you, soon picked his nose (though not literally) to ridicule. But how ugly was Matt? What's the evidence? The fact that many readers of this book could have kissed him on various occasions doesn't really count I guess, but quite seriously, the 'ugly' claim has been – in my opinion – rather a consequence of jumpers, haircuts and spite than actual hideousness. He's actually a bit of a looker really in a footballing context! Now these guys (below) were *really* ugly – Matty, I shall argue not for the first or last time in this book – is different class.

Iain Dowie. Apparently thought himself to be a bit of a looker. One can only quote Dangermouse on such occasions: 'Good grief!'. Most people go to the supermarket for sour cream. Iain just looks at milk.

Peter Beardsley. Such a nice man and such a talented footballer. Apparently a devoted father although how his Quasimodo looks have been allowed or able to be further perpetuated in humanity's gene pool is something of a mystery.

Luke Chadwick. Relatively inexperienced compared to Dowie and Beardsley but no one can deny that he has fallen from the ugly tree and hit every single branch on the way down. Fortunately for him one can quote Ruby Wax on such occasions, since he is 'now earning the kind of cash that'll open any woman's legs.'

Ewan Roberts – actually, you'd probably quite fancy him in a room with Dowie and Chadwick but ginger and toothless have never really done it for anyone.

Dave Beasant – no, not really, but he fancies himself enough to aggravate him by putting him in. So if you read this and know him, let him know that he's the fifth ugliest footballer of all time.

Ronaldo – doesn't help himself with ridiculous haircuts but what a fantastic chipmunk impression. Ronaldo is Brazilian for chipmunk incidentally.

Ronaldinho is Brazilian for little chipmunk and he does an even better chipmunk impression than Ronaldo.

Maradona – Jabba the Hutt. Maradona has always been right up there in popularity terms for me. Augusto Pinochet, Jim Davidson and Thatcher are amongst those of equal standing but whatever you think of him it is extraordinary that his growth rate has exceeded Andy Goram next to a plate of cream cakes.

That all-over-body-hair bloke who played left back for Bulgaria and who no one was quite sure was actually human.

David Fairclough – so ugly Liverpool only ever risked putting him on the field for 5 minutes.

Teddy Sheringham – in a 'Dorian Gray' sense.

I'd have liked to add some others such as Kenny Burns but was too scared. Apologies for any obvious omissions – Martin Keown comes to mind at this very moment.

Those who subscribe to the 'Matt was his own worst enemy' story may be interested in his account of how and why he didn't go to Spurs where Terry Venables was manager at the time. Apparently, Le Tiss had actually agreed to the move and then changed his mind because he didn't want to leave Southampton (fair enough!). Having conveyed this change of heart through his agent, the agent rang back to say he had Terry on the line wanting to talk things through. So did Matty say, 'I'm sorry Mr Venables, I've changed my mind and will not change it back. Sorry again but that's how things are sometimes. No hard feelings I hope'? Err...actually no! Matty said to his agent that he wouldn't even speak to Venables: 'I've made my decision – he can sod off!' was the gist of his argument. Now how was he to know El Tel would become England manager one day?

Although in retrospect Le Tissier might have left the Saints at that point, the same is also true of the time under Ian Branfoot (because it was Ian Branfoot), or in Le Tissier's golden period (because everyone wanted him) or while Hoddle was England manager (because it must have been clear by then that getting picked for England whilst at Southampton was not easy). He might even have left after that, as it became clear that regular first team football might only be possible at that stage through a move to somewhere like Bournemouth (no disrespect intended) or even the ultimate indignity of Portsmouth (disrespect intended). In short, Le Tissier's loyalty is nothing short of absolutely remarkable. So, as the gangly youth became something really special so that even 'big clubs' (ho ho!) like Spurs wanted him, he still stayed with the Saints and thus benefited from the motivational and coaching skills of a certain Ian Branfoot. The good times were about to roll! (Er...not!)

Chapter 3:

The Branfoot Years

The story is told that Ian Branfoot agreed to swap Robert Fleck for Le Tissier, except Saints would also have to pay half a million. This is possibly a good deal. Maybe as good as when Blackburn said, 'we can't quite afford £7 million for Kevin Davies, why don't you take £6 million and James Beattie as well?' Maybe *even* as good a deal as when my wife assured me that Safeways had some excellent '3 for the price of 4' offers. Whatever the truth of the Fleck story, it probably tells you all you need to know about this sorry sordid little chapter about one of the least talked about managers in conversations about great managers.

Mind Trick

Completely unconnected to that first paragraph of course, I would now like to hazard a guess as to what kinds of words have just come to the mind of any Saints fan reading this: arrogant, useless, twat, tosser, w*****, c***, f***wit would be my guesses. Was I right? Proper little Uri Gellar/Paul Daniels me!

It may or may not be true that Le Tissier refused to discuss the Fleck 'deal' (or rather 'insult') on the grounds that he would 'see you [Branfoot] out of here' but he certainly didn't go, and when asked about the period makes it clear that *him* moving was not necessary when crowds had nosedived to less than 50% of capacity, making Branfoot's exit a certainty. It may also be true, or not, that Branfoot was visited by the ghost of Pompey past in a dream, and warned that if he really wanted to be the most unpopular Saints manager of all time he would really have to go some: 'Beware of one who is to come...' Although that does seem entirely the most likely explanation of his appalling decision making and motivational skills, unless Mr Branfoot really was simply an arrogant, useless tosser. But how likely is that? His record speaks for itself.

Indeed, Ian Branfoot has received plenty of press coverage over the years and it has to be said that not all of it was entirely justified. I say that not all of it was entirely justified because sometimes journalists found something positive to say. Branfoot probably liked to consider himself a pragmatist; if you combine with that dumb arrogance and the decision – world-class player or no world-class player – that Saints needed to play with a certain style, which amounted to playing without any style at all ... then all of this was not good news for the young Le Tiss.

For an unsophisticated (though admittedly *very* talented) battering ram in the 'style' of Alan Shearer, this actually worked out rather well, allowing him to establish a reputation and earn a big money transfer to Blackburn. However, once Shearer's crude but effective skills had gone, the flaw in Branfoot's plan became clear – to work at all it needed better players than Saints had available. Terry Hurlock hoofing to Paul Moody is not going to out-fox even the worst defences, let alone the best. Old-timers like David Speedie and Kerry Dixon just weren't good enough either, although Ian 'football genius' Branfoot reckoned they would score more than Shearer in the season after he left the Saints. If he had not found the net *at all* for Blackburn (which he actually managed to do 22 times), Branfoot would have been right for once – but only just!

Le Tissier's record under Branfoot is actually pretty good for a midfielder/striker who was under-valued and dropped. In Branfoot's 2 full seasons as manager at The Dell in 1991/92, Matty scored 15 times in 50 matches (including the goals that took Saints to the highly prestigious Zenith

Data Systems Cup Final) and an impressive 18 in 43 the following year. That's a goal every three games overall. Even so, as calls for Branfoot's head became louder in 1993/94 it was Le Tissier whom Branfoot tried to make the scapegoat, dropping him for 5 games in the autumn during which time – of course – Saints failed to win. When Le Tissier then returned to win the next match single-handedly, rather than Branfoot admitting his error he tried to claim the credit. In fact, and despite being wrong so consistently, he has continued to claim he was right to drop Matty to this day. (And they say Matty's self-belief was something else!)

Win Bonus

It often seems that footballers are either grafters for the team (David Batty) or potentially brilliant but not liked for their attitude (Nicolas Anelka). Whatever the press might say about his laziness, as long as their win bonuses relied exclusively on Le Tissier being in the team – as happened for seasons on end – Matty's team-mates didn't have a problem with his work-rate.

But whilst Branfoot simply demonstrates an irritating arrogance which he was even willing to commit to Le Tissier's testimonial programme, it is in fact extraordinary that with a manager like Branfoot doing his best to crush Matty's confidence, and with the team eschewing footballing style in favour of the 'hoof', Le Tissier was able to maintain total confidence in his own ability. It is also extraordinary that, with Rod Wallace leaving for Leeds at the end of 1990-91 and Shearer a year later, Le Tissier didn't just say 'sod ya' and accept he wasn't quite as good as Robert Fleck (who?).

As stories have since emerged of who was trying to sign him, and for how much of a pay rise, it becomes absolutely incredible that he stayed at Southampton, surely setting Matty apart in any era of football. Quality of life *is* important, yes, but I'm sure many reading this would agree that if your manager at work is a complete idiot it is actually quite difficult to have a good quality of life, however much you earn. And in fact, however nice Hampshire is, I'm sure many would also agree that other locations in the UK (not to mention the south of France, Catalan coast, Italian lakes etc.) also offer very attractive locations and lifestyles, especially for the rich and the famous.

It was, then, extraordinary that a team with one win and seven defeats should drop their top scorer from the previous season and quite obviously their best player. It is even more extraordinary that when the team finally struggled to a win when that player was recalled, the manager had the gall to say, 'told you so.' (Only a change of manager and Matt's brilliance allowed Saints ultimately to survive that little experiment.) But no one was fooled; the game against Newcastle was – despite Branfoot's attempts to claim the credit – almost the final nail in his managerial coffin, with FA Cup exit providing the finishing touch. The difference Le Tissier made in that game just went to show that if Branfoot had been *any* sort of manager he wouldn't have dropped Le Tissier to get the best from him, he would have got what he needed from him anyway, as absolutely essential to Saints success. Even a manager as limited as Alan Ball was to prove that possible! Waving red cards and banners, singing 'how could you leave him out?' was the justifiable response from those Saints fans who hadn't already voted against Branfoot's hideously ugly brand of football with their feet.

I was there that day – armed with my 'red card' for Ian – and it took Le Tissier 19 whole seconds to dribble around a couple of defenders and shoot. Within a few minutes more he had turned up again dangerously in the penalty area and then done one of his juggling tricks which – while they may not be shown as much as his goals – delighted his fans and made an appearance almost every time he played (even those where he allegedly did 'nothing'). Still within the first 20 minutes a delicate Le Tissier header guided the ball into

Paul Allen's path setting him free on goal. Although his shot was poor, it was actually so poor that it became a good cross, presenting an open goal that Shearer would have devoured in an instant. Iain Dowie on the other hand (bless him, he tried, he really did) swung a hopeful boot which made contact with nothing, and the moment was gone. As the commentator suggested, as Iain's boot went flying into the opposition just a few moments later, 'if he'd made half as much contact with the ball a moment ago as he did with Beardsley just then...'

In fact, in the hour of the game before Le Tissier scored the goals that made it famous, several times he effected instant controls and picked out team-mates with passes of various lengths, invariably putting the ball in their stride and setting Saints on the attack. In retrospect it seems even more remarkable that he was playing for Southampton. Other sides would have given him the ball more had he played for them; their tactics and players would have allowed it. If Le Tissier's inch-perfect assists earlier in the Newcastle game had, instead, fallen to Scholes or Shearer rather than Allen and Dowie, two goals would surely have resulted. But here was Le Tissier playing for a team that struggled to get the ball in the first place, and then found it easy to give away again. Given the Beckham/Real Madrid stuff, Matty's loyalty would be incredible even if he had played for

Manchester United, but for a team where his riches were not only unappreciated by managers like Branfoot and Souness but also squandered by hard-working but limited 'co-workers', it is incredible. Le Tiss got by with *very* little help from his friends, however much his own modesty would recognise that their toil was crucial. If you transfer it to your own work situation, you know you'd have been out of the door however good the city/location.

If Saints got the ball in that game Le Tissier had promised something. But – in support of the above contention – most of the time Saints did *not* get the ball at all. Newcastle were totally dominant that day and it must be said that if Shearer had been playing for them then, at half-time, they would have been 3 up. If *Matty* had been playing for them, they'd have been 5 up! I remember saying at half-time – it was 0-0 – that we'd win 2-1 with 2 goals from Matty. This was partly optimistic as well as prophetic, but actually based more on logic than simply blind faith. The fact was Saints *had* to play better in the second half, and had had so much luck so far that perhaps this was their day – that's what makes football the game it is and one of the reasons Americans don't understand it. Additionally, if I was right that Saints must improve, even then it would only be Le Tissier who was good enough to unlock the defences of good teams for the Saints. Even in the first half, when his critics would probably say he didn't do much because he didn't lay on 3 goals and score 4 more whilst juggling swords and reciting Mercutio's death scene from *Romeo and Juliet*, he nevertheless almost scored after 19 seconds and then again just before half-time as well as being the source of any rare moments worthy of applause from Southampton fans.

I have seen the goals so often on television that I almost forget what it was like to be there, in the lower east stand just near where Dowie's misplaced knock-down from Kevin Moore started it all. But however much the memory fades of that chilly November afternoon I'm glad I didn't take the easy option of viewing on Sky. Not just because I can say I saw the greatest goal ever and say 'I know 'cos I was there' à la Max Boyce, but because the TV commentary was so frankly nauseating that I would have thrown something at the set. Admittedly, no commentator is going to say 'few lucky bounces and then a tap in past the keeper', but in other respects Andy Gray and Martin Tyler did their best to run down one of the great moments and players in football. 'You watch and you wonder and you think he's lazy and lethargic and then this happens,' mused Tyler viewing the replay. What! Well actually, 'no, none of the above.' I wasn't thinking any of that. How about 'you watch *in* wonder.' There followed a dialogue about how *brave* Ian Branfoot was to drop Le Tiss in the first place and how –

never mind Saints' pathetic league position – he had been even braver to 'risk' recalling him. I often wonder – given the unreasonable extremes of feeling amongst some Saints fans (death threats etc.) – whether TV felt a bit sorry for Branfoot? *That* would be entirely understandable – but giving credit for one person's skill to another's singular incapacity to get things right is not.

Ian Branfoot's reaction to the goal was, or at least appears to have been, one of annoyance more than anything else. No celebration, no smile – just an irritated turn to his left to bark at Paul Moody (ready to appear as a substitute) to 'sit down Moods'. Claims were made at the time that Saints were *not* about to bring on Moody for Le Tiss. But then again what manager would proudly proclaim 'you know that bloke I dropped for 5 games? You know while we couldn't get a win? Well he has just scored the most sublime goal ever and I was just about to substitute him in favour of the 'goal-scoring' stick insect from Waterlooville.' Even the great comedy circus act himself could think quicker than that, but despite any post hoc justification of which substitution was planned, Branfoot's reaction suggests something different. After all if he'd taken Le Tiss off and then Saints had won that would really have got his critics thinking...but of course Saints just didn't win (ever) without Matt – something he consistently appears to have forgotten. Branfoot's 'explanation' in Le Tissier's own testimonial is interesting to say the least. At the time the Saints bench quickly said that they weren't going to substitute Le Tissier; but now Branfoot says: 'I honestly can't remember. My memory's absolutely awful.' Yeah right. The case for the prosecution rests.

The goal itself is probably worth a paragraph. In fact, probably worth an electronic version of this book with a clickable link to footage, preferably without the Sky commentary. Dowie's header down (from a long hoof obviously) went behind Le Tissier who, nonetheless, managed to flick it back over his head and into his own path with his left foot, and then instantly over an on-rushing Barry Venison. As it came to ground again, the outside of the right boot was used again to take the ball over and inside the centre-half, Kevin Scott, presenting Le God – to the left of the penalty spot – with Mike Hooper in the Mags' goal. The side-foot volley was not crisply struck, as Matt modestly concedes, but that hardly matters given that control and accuracy were what was needed and provided. I went wild. Everyone went wild. I told you so. We *all* told you so! You *see*, Branfoot? It was all too much. The second before the goal seemed to last forever. So many thoughts went through your head: I'm seeing *this* at Southampton? This is Le Tiss v Branfoot...wouldn't it be awful if he misses now ...

but he won't miss. And he didn't, and just before the celebration there was almost a fraction of a second of disbelief. A feeling of fantastic satisfaction. We had scored plus Matty had scored plus one of the greatest goals ever plus 'we want Branfoot out' were all rolled up into the emotional celebration.

Perhaps that was almost Branfoot's last game anyway. Imagine defeat when the player you had dropped had done that?! But that's almost what happened as Newcastle continued to test Flowers and the woodwork, and as Andy Cole continued to prove why his own England claims were rather less worthy than Matty's own. But in the end Cole did, finally, manage to tuck one away, before squandering other chances to win it. Again, the commentary is instructive. Whilst they are 'watching and wondering' and thinking Le Tissier is lazy, apparently Andy Cole's 'movement is sensational' and 'good strikers will tell you they only worry when they're not getting the chances not when they're missing them.' But Cole misses and misses and misses; surely they/he must worry a bit! Why do the commentators not say 'you watch and you wonder and you think f***ing hell when's the cart-horse gonna take one f' Chissake?!' But anyway, he did finally equalise, taking one of the 10 open goals he'd had, which is about the ratio I really would expect from my grandmother, despite her dodgy left knee and proclivity to stray into offside positions because she can't carry her tea quickly enough. Furthermore, on this particular day, Cole's 'great movement' even allowed him to be standing around the penalty spot, 8 yards offside, while Rob Lee curled a 31st minute shot into the top corner from outside the box. It may have gone in anyway, but as it passed within a few feet of the stranded Cole it had to be disallowed.

And so, of course, to Le Tissier's second which I hesitate to describe as a 'lazy' volley. The fact is that so many times I have watched Le Tissier and he makes everything look so easy. The same spherical object which when it hit Carlton Palmer (being 'hit' being his preferred method of ball-control) bounced halfway to Bournemouth, hit Matty's thigh or instep and dropped exactly where he wanted it to. It is easy to take that instant control for granted but how many times does Andy Gray comment that the first touch has taken a player too wide and let the chance go begging? On this occasion, Neil Maddison's close-range downward header 'hit' Le Tissier's thigh, bouncing up and in the direction of goal, allowing his right leg to swing round like a graceful pendulum sending the ball up and over Hooper and into the far corner of the net. It looks simple and easy because it's so natural, but lazy *would* be the wrong word. Very definitely the wrong word. This time Branfoot did manage a smile, but it did not look like the smile of a manager who has just won 3 points, or of someone who had been proved conclusively wrong. It looked more like the wry, resigned (why didn't he?) smile of someone who thinks that those efforts may actually have weakened his own position. True, if Le Tissier did that every week Branfoot would have probably kept his job. But if the manager had no influence on how often a player did that kind of thing then you could put me in charge. Or anyone. Or a gazelle, mouldy star-fruit, packet of spangles, blob of mucus etc. – you get the picture. And then Saints hung on. For once. Despite the time of the goal it was another 7 or 8 minutes including injury time before Branfoot realised that he needed to claim the credit.

To write so much on that one game is understandable in the context of the Branfoot era as it seems to say so much about it. Top scorer in 1992/93 and ZDS Cup Final scorer in 1991/92 notwithstanding, this is the period in Matty's career where a promising youngster ought really to have made big strides. It makes the decisions of young players today moving to bigger clubs more intelligible, and Matty's loyalty the more remarkable, but the Branfoot years really do seem to have labelled Le Tiss unnecessarily. Playing in a tactically and technically weak team, struggling against relegation, shifting most of its best young players, signing mostly poor or old ones, it seems that what might have been the start of something big, was in fact the time when Matty is labelled lazy. He is a luxury. Even when new management subsequently encourages him to score 25, even 30 goals in a season it is a tag he struggled to get rid of. The curse of the Branfoot, it appears, is that Matty doesn't get in on the England ground floor à la Gascoigne, and that a player who apparently 'struggles' to get in the Saints team is hardly felt good enough to base a national team around. The curse of the Hoddle (the player) is that future managers – even Hoddle himself – fail to see the possibilities. Still, Di Canio never played for Italy, so it's not just us!

People are loath to admit their mistakes, and so for a long time the Southampton board stuck with Branfoot. Presumably each Le Tiss-inspired win helped them believe a corner was being turned, but in the end, as attendances dropped into 4 figures they had a commercial reason for ditching the genius of Ian which did not necessarily imply a footballing mistake. And one wonders in those two-and-a-half years if attendances might not have fallen even further if it wasn't for those bits of Le Tiss magic. He really did justify the admission fee in those days. Playing away in Portsmouth blue (so was Branfoot *really* a Pompey plot? That would explain things!) Nottingham Forest seemed to be particularly victimised, with Le Tiss regularly finding the net at the Trent End. Still he tried to make amends by missing his only penalty against them, only to undo that good work by lashing home a thunderous left-foot volley against them in the same game – one of his finest, and perhaps most underrated strikes?

Although other crowds were to do the same – most notably at Ewood Park a few years later – one of the most memorable moments came at Anfield where the recently recalled Le Tissier not only totally bamboozled Mark Wright before firing home a left-foot volley, but earned a round of applause from The Kop for doing so. Most football fans would concede how special something would need to be in the eyes of the opposition before they would actually put their hands together in appreciation of a goal.

So, it might be too extreme to say that Ian Branfoot was the making of Alan Shearer and the end of Matty, but he certainly had a big influence on their respective careers. Always impressive, but without that supportive hand which might have helped him reach his potential, Le Tissier failed to threaten England selection seriously at this time. Though, as we shall see, what he subsequently achieved is often quite brilliant, it might have been so much more. Shearer on the other hand, and no doubt also through his own hard work and ambition, had the platform for much more. As Le Tissier consistently out-scored Shearer in their time together at Saints, one wonders whether the same could have happened for England. More, one wonders how many they might have scored given the opportunity to play together. Certainly when one remembers the 'great' England side of 1992-94 it makes you weep!

Chapter 4:

One-Man Team

My own involvement with the Saints coincided with the golden, or perhaps that ought to be platinum, period in Matty's Southampton career, although I know of no one who was there from the start who shares a different opinion from mine. Of course prior to 1994 Le Tissier had already scored some cracking goals, been Southampton's player of the year and PFA young player of the year, attracted the interest of various other clubs and established himself a reputation as a deadly penalty-taker. I had seen the sublime and the ridiculous from him already in my odd trip to The Dell. Among my earliest memories are a deflected shot to beat Liverpool 1-0, the laziest and most comical attempt ever at a header I have ever seen (flicking his hair at the ball from what seemed like 15 yards away) and the nutmegging of John Barnes for seemingly no other reason than to show off, given that it had looked easy to get in a cross ages before Barnes arrived on the scene.

Donkey

Incidentally, I also remember in one of my early matches at The Dell a sensational miss by Alan Shearer from 6 yards when it seemed it would have been easier to climb Mount Everest, creosote a fence around the entire perimeter of Yorkshire and *then* come back and score. I accept that Alan has made the best of his career and I have been pleased to see him in an England shirt, but I have far more memories of Le Tissier and Le Tissier scored far more goals when they played together.

Looking back on the days when he eclipsed Shearer week in, week out, Matty has noted how much Shearer worked at his game. Shearer putting in loads of extra practice whilst Le Tiss himself rarely did so, unless forced to do extra training by frustrated (but obviously wrong) managers. Indeed apart from creosoting fences it is hard to imagine Shearer having more *natural* flair at anything. But given the ultimate record of relatively untalented ones like Shearer, Le Tiss does concede in retrospect that there is a case that he didn't make enough of his career, or rather that he could have achieved more. Whatever! I would nonetheless maintain the case that if others had shown in him the same faith as he had in himself, as Alan Ball had and however many 1000s in Southampton had, then things might have been very different all the same.

Lion

'Have you ever staked out a water hole in the African bush? It is extremely exciting. You get there tremendously early, and you sit there for hours and hours and *absolutely nothing* happens. And yet you never look away because you know that, if you did, you would miss something so ridiculously wonderful you will never forget it. It's not about what happens, it's about what might happen. If you wish to duplicate this experience without the trouble and expense of going to Africa I suggest you become a Southampton supporter. Or put it another way, a Le Tissier supporter. He remains the most compelling footballer in England because of what he *might* do ... No other player conveys that sense of almost limitless possibility.' Simon Barnes, *The Guardian*, 1996.

Prior to 1993 I had shown Le Tissiesque loyalty, and for even longer than Matt's 17 years, in supporting my local non-league team, Bishop's Stortford FC. I had seen them win Cup Finals at Wembley (FA Amateur Cup 1974 and FA Trophy 1981) and, even in the relatively miserable times of the late 80s and early 90s (relegation from Isthmian Premier) I had chugged around the outskirts of London in a Mini Metro called 'Betty Boo' (from Southampton) to places like Sutton, Hayes, Aylesbury and Enfield. I still watch them now. But in the period 1993-1996 I became almost exclusively a Le Tissier fan and no-one could convince me that England didn't miss an important opportunity in this period. At that time, and despite some affection for Southampton, I would probably have stopped supporting them if Le Tiss had left; which is frightening because he might have gone to Tottenham Hotspur! (Shudders at potential implication.) In any case, whatever the 'ifs' and 'buts' this was a very special time. Southampton stayed in the Premiership – just – thanks almost exclusively to the efforts of one man.

Saying that, Alan Ball does deserve some credit for Southampton surviving in the Premiership in 1993/94, of course. He did, after all, manage to do what Ian Branfoot had not managed to do and realise that the only way that particular team was going to survive was to ensure that it made the most of its one true quality, creative player. This seems a somewhat obvious thing to do, but the other option had been rather to sign a selection of ungainly giraffes, shuffling buffalo and variously sized over-aged donkeys and then getting pensioners to clog the ball at them. Other managers than Ball could have recognised the flaws in the latter and strengths of the former, one suspects ... however, many did not, and Le Tissier recalls the times when he was recalled effectively with the task of scoring goals to save someone their job. But for Alan Ball, although he foolishly made the mistake of believing Manchester City to be a big club (only joking guys!) a little later, Matty kept his job more than secure. In his initial half-season, Ball's enthusiastic 'fan-like' endorsement of Matty made all the difference and, despite losing 23 of 42 games (a record number of losses for a surviving team in the top division, I believe, very many of which were under Branfoot), Saints managed to win enough to survive on the last day. (Le Tissier notes on the 1993/94 goals video that he hopes 'we' never put you through that again. (1) As if! (2) I think a look at the facts suggests that without Matty a very 'comfortable' lowest ever points season would likely have ensued. In this period Saints only ever picked up binary points when Le Tiss was absent.)

So Alan Ball made a reasonable managerial decision. You can't lose 'em all, I guess. But of course most of the credit should go to Le Tissier himself. The scale of his achievement is awesome. As well as his 25 goals in 1993/94 in the games he played (having been dropped by Branfoot for five games and suspended at one point), he was involved in assists in over 60% of the other goals Saints scored – whilst those other goals in fact did not total anywhere near as many as his own contribution. After Ball took over, the extent of the one-man team became truly extraordinary with Le Tissier at the heart of everything. Ball's team talks must have been blindingly simple: 'Matty takes the corners, Matty takes the free-kicks, Matty scores the goals. Everyone else wins the ball and gives it to Matty.' (I bet he regrets going to Manchester City; they may have done too!). Jason Dodd is quoted in Le Tissier's testimonial magazine as saying, 'My early career was a case of "pass the ball to Matty and he'll do the rest!"' Many a true word spoken in jest.

As mentioned in the introduction to this book, towards the season's end only one Saints goal was not either scored, or laid on, by Le Tissier. That was an own goal by Robert Ullathorne at Norwich, now a mainstay of Notts County's attempts to be no longer the oldest football *league* club. However, to make up for his lack of involvement (the unfortunate Ullathorne deflecting in a Neil Maddison shot) Le Tiss scored the second with his left, the third through a penalty and the 4th with his head.

My Left Foot

As an aside, it is remarkable how often Le Tissier found the net with other than his favoured foot. Though it was clearly his stronger, Le Tissier rarely wasted time trying to get the ball onto his right foot, unless to out-fox an opponent, whether crossing or shooting. Thus he was often able to save time and take opportunities a less confident player might have missed. The confidence to use his left foot allowed him to score spectacular goals like the volley against Forest in 1992/93 (to make amends for his one and only penalty miss in the same game), or to put in the left-foot cross whilst running away from goal which set up Dowie in the crucial Blackburn game at the end of the 1993/94 season. A 'natural left-footer', as Trevor Brooking would put it despite my puerile sniggering, would struggle to match either bit of skill.

Returning to that Norwich game, for good measure Le Tiss also planted a corner onto Ken Monkou's head in the 90th minute; Saints won 4-5 with Monkou giving Saints the lead for the first time before throwing the ball into the travelling support – an act so ridiculous it still makes me smile. Failure to win *that* game would have been enough to see Saints relegated.

Southampton's final two home games of the season were extraordinary – and among the first Saints games I had to pay to get into. The first was against Blackburn, chasing the championship. In retrospect the 'creditable draw' that I guess most Saints fans would have settled for would not have been enough to save the team from relegation. But they didn't have to settle for that. In the first half Le Tissier's incredible left-foot cross (mentioned above) allowed Dowie to head home. A little later a defence-splitting pass allowed in Paul Allen for 2-0 (do I really need to add whose was the defence-splitting pass?) 2-0 half-time. But in the second half Blackburn were initially all over Southampton. Stuart Ripley scored at The Dell (not something which ever happened when he played for Saints, but then Dave Beasant wasn't always around for the assist) and at 1-2 Blackburn pressed strongly for the equaliser which it seemed almost certain they would get. The tension was unbearable; slightly the worse for wear I could think of no other coping mechanism than to scream 'Judas' at an annoyingly loud volume and pitch if ever Shearer came near. One such occasion was when Saints broke away and earned a rare corner. Matty swung it in and a towering header – I forget from whom (Monkou?) – hit Tim Sherwood smack bang in the very centre (I mean exactly to the centimetre) of his chest, before then bouncing harmlessly through to the keeper, Flowers. The referee, not unreasonably in my view, gave a penalty. Chest ball!

I say 'not unreasonably' because by this stage I had worked myself up into a George Bush Junior-style frenzy. A mixture of the old 'drinking' Bush and the new 'apologist for butchery' Bush, I was by that time regarding this fixture as the epitome of the perpetual struggle between good and evil. In the evil corner, the moneybags 'new football'. And in the other corner, representing good, the old-fashioned local team, The, quite literally, Saints. It was the spiteful Shearer ('one greedy b******' – not to mention smug and gloating) against the overlooked saviour. As Matty placed the ball on the spot, Alan had a few 'friendly' words with him. The ball of righteous fury that I had become and which was growing, screamed insanely: 'Judas!' What a pleasure I must have been to stand next to. (Wife's Note: He was!)

Finally, as Shearer was encouraged to depart by the referee, Le Tissier calmly took the penalty. Unfortunately there can be no drama in describing it because of course he scored, as usual, before himself having a few words with the other ex-Saint in goal, Timmy Flowers. Bedlam. Good had triumphed over evil. 'He' was leading us to salvation. And he did! Against Villa in the next home fixture, the exquisite touch and super-accurate corners again led to a comfortable 4-1 win, followed up by a free-kick to silence the 'he's got a f****** big nosers', a penalty and a 'little dance taking the piss' before putting the ball on Maddison's head v West Ham in the final match of the season. 3-3. Saints safe by a point, although having slid into the relegation zone at one point that day.

The 1994/95 season was similar in a number of ways, although after too many draws and the usual flirt with relegation Saints eventually managed to finish 10th. This time Matty 'chipped in' with a mere 30 goals and other players too managed a few more – although again Le Tissier was responsible for over 50% of the goals he didn't score, through assists. Memorably, in the FA Cup replay against Luton, John Motson was working himself up into a right lather of adulation for Le Tissier's skill. As the ball came to Matty just outside the penalty area Motson excitedly squealed, 'I wonder what he's going to do *this* time?' Then, as a cross-field pass found neither the centre-forward with a cross, nor the net with a shot, Motson issued an odd sound: a stifled groan of disappointment. At this point enter Neil Heaney, emerging from 'nowhere' and crashing in a diving header at the far post as part of a Le Tiss-orchestrated 6-0 win. Motson then emitted another kind of low-pitched moaning noise, which one can only assume to have been some kind of sexual climax.

I have to say I probably came close (pun intended) to achieving such a 'memorable Motty moment' in December

1994. Sky had changed a Saints home game from the Saturday to the Monday – not much good if you have to be in York on the Monday and have arranged to see friends in Southampton on the Saturday...not that I suppose Sky care about the countless times they've done that to people. So, after a football-less weekend in Southampton, I found myself watching Saints v Villa in a pretty empty York pub on a cold Monday night. I had managed to drag along some fellow conference attendees – something which in retrospect may not have been such a good idea. Southampton took an early lead through Richard Hall's towering header (from a Le Tissier corner of course) and despite being largely outplayed seemed to be heading for 3 probably undeserved points.

I remember hating almost every minute of the game. Indeed from the current perspective – after a few seasons of finishing 8th or 10th – it is easy to forget that in those days (which have returned as I check the manuscript) every game was a relegation battle and every 3 points priceless. In fact, even if we qualified for the Champions League every season, I still think I'd be assessing the permutations and preparing for the glorious day on which to play 'Mathematically Safe' by Half Man Half Biscuit (which may not be possible by the time this book is produced). Accordingly, somewhat anxious, between our 6th minute lead and 82nd minute capitulation in the form of a Ray Houghton equaliser, I had been heavily stress-drinking.

Through the drunken haze it had now seemed inevitable that Villa would get a winner. Dreams of 3 points had, instead, turned to desperate prayers that we might hold on for one. In the 91st minute Villa had a reasonable penalty appeal – one of those 'seen 'em given' types – and having survived that it was a relief as Saints punted the ball up-field and won a somewhat dubious free-kick the wrong side of 30 yards out. Whilst of course my estimate of '30 yards' is probably ruled by the footballing convention of believing a yard to be about 75 centimetres, even so it certainly seemed to be both the 'wrong side' and too far out for even Le Tiss. Even so, getting the wall in position and back meant that this would almost certainly be the last kick of the game, although this was in the days before the board for minimum added minutes. 91 minutes and 52 seconds, 53 seconds, 54 ... Le Tissier stepped up...

Perhaps Nigel Spink in the Villa goal thought it too far out and wrong side as well, because although the shot was good it was far from in the very corner and perhaps it should have been saved. But it wasn't. It flew in off the keeper's despairing, unconvincing diving effort. I remember howling and cheering; rolling around and screaming, kneeling before the table and bashing my fists on it, wailing, 'yes,

yes'. I was almost crying as I rushed to order another pint for myself and pleaded for the final whistle, which was actually a few more kicks away than I would have liked. The few people in the pub couldn't imagine what I was feeling, although perhaps they could because the answer was mostly 'drunk'. I think they were actually plain embarrassed, but I cared not until the morning. Two goals to one after really not convincing. Le Tissier, one goal, one assist. How often that happened.

Watching the game again later, Andy Gray's commentary had asked, 'can I change my man of the match?', whilst Le Tissier himself just stood and looked around – like Don Bradman without the bat acknowledging another 100 – as if to say, 'did you ever doubt me?' Indeed it is probably during these genius years that Le Tiss finally got into some kind of rhythm in terms of goal celebrations. Not for Matty the Shearer 'gloat' or the Channon 'arm-swinging'. In the early years Matty went through a series of goal celebrations, some more successful than others. A fist-clenched salute whilst half-kneeling, which seemed to be reserved for The Dell's Milton Road, was quite impressive, but the little skips and limp high fives that accompanied other goals were less so. By the time of the Villa game, however, I think he had found 'the one', although he didn't always use it. He just stood still, looking around at the faithful (and oh how we all believed) and let everyone else jump on him. Lazy? Nah, just conserving energy.

Oddly enough, after umpteen draws in umpteen +1 games, Le Tiss himself suggests that Saints' turning-point was a 3-1 win against Newcastle in the spring, which was remarkable for a number of reasons. First, Saints were losing 0-1 from the 17th to the 86th minute. It may only happen once in a lifetime but this was payback time for the people who stay with their team to the bitter end. Their reward. As the moaners and the 'come on, let's miss the traffic' brigades streamed away from The Dell, for once it was not Le Tiss who single-handedly saved the Saints. No, this time the hands responsible were those of Pavel Srnicek, who by all accounts had had a decent game to that point. And so with no goals or assists for Le Tissier and several late-game blunders by the Newcastle keeper, Southampton won. (Watching that game with the time-delay of Ceefax was agony; at one point I knew the game must actually be over, and the score on the screen still said 1-0 to Newcastle. It was odd waiting for Ceefax to catch up!)

One might actually argue that there were other turning-points, most notably snatching a point at home to West Ham in the previous game, but in any case, aided by 30-goal Matt, Saints were headed for mid-table respectability

– a phrase incidentally used by Angus Loughran (Statto) on that season's goals video around 30 times! Perhaps the finest hour came in a Sky-televised 4-3 win over Spurs just after Venables had overlooked Le Tiss again for England. David Pleat – why do they let him commentate? – was grudging and patronising in attempting 'kind of' to recognise that Le Tissier's 2 goals and an assist actually did mean he was quite an influential player – 'if only he could get more involved' he whined. If he could get more involved in each game than 2 goals and an assist, Southampton would have replaced Manchester United as team of the decade. (And as a footnote, I would just like to add, 'Thanks for gloating at Archer's Road following your goal, Teddy Sheringham – we all agree with Arsenal fans' particular Anglo-Saxon appraisal of you.' You *are* still one.)

In some senses it may seem odd to go as far as 1995/96 in thinking about Matt's 'genius' years; the years that he was a one-man team. But it was, in many ways, a quite extraordinary season. First, a man who had scored 25 and 30 goals, from midfield, for a struggling side in the previous two years, not only failed to be an automatic choice for the national team but was hardly in serious contention for an England place at all. Second, Alan Ball left for Manchester City and managed to get them just enough points, but not enough goals, so that they were relegated on the season's final day on goal difference with Saints being the team that just stayed up instead. In a remarkable demonstration of how much Ball struggled managerially when the tactics required went beyond 'give it to Matty', he even had his new team time-wasting in the last ten minutes when only a goal would have saved them. In the words of one E Cartman of Southpark, Colorado, 'revenge is so very, very sweet.'

The fact that England clearly weren't going to give Matty a real chance was demoralising to say the least to his many fans. How much more so it must have been to Matt, and might be used as an argument for explaining a relative decline in form. Some have made this argument. Even so, as Saints toiled and scraped their way to an unlikely relegation escape, it was still Matty's class which finally told and which, despite the tension of the final day of that season, always gave me some kind of insane hope of salvation. The 'decline', such as it was, still saw Matty claim double figures from midfield. And he *still* came up with the goods when it really mattered. Apart from anything else he was involved – as non-scorer – in around half Saints' goals, the vast majority of these being direct assists, with his total of assists exceeding the previous year. In short, in a season where Saints struggled to find the net much more than in the previous season, Matty was *once again* nonetheless involved in 75-80% of Southampton's total number of goals. The rest did score a few goals when he was injured or suspended, but looked woefully impotent and unable to register Premiership points in other than multiples of one – if that.

After an opening-day hat-trick against Nottingham Forest, as Saints slumped to a 3-4 defeat, Le Tissier failed to get on the Premiership scoresheet again until April. But then his goal to win the match against Bolton at Burnden Park and key role in the victory over Manchester United were what kept the Saints alive. In the United match, his ability to make Peter Schmeichel (that doesn't look right but I'm not looking it up) look like a hapless drunk-driver looking for their keys on a car-park floor, were especially amusing. Although in the final game – 0-0 against Wimbledon – he couldn't score the goal to ensure Saints' absolute safety, the fact is that the Saints *were* safe, and in a poor season for goals it was his which had been crucial in the end. Apart from a spell in late February and March, Le Tissier's contribution was still outstanding and crucial with a full quarter-century of assists. Although ultimately frustrating as a season for a player who had been used to scoring more often, he made the difference. His clinical assists in 1-0 victories v Newcastle and Coventry and goals in 1-0 victories v Blackburn (converting the penalty his own through-ball had made inevitable) and Bolton made all the difference for a team which collected just 38 points in total.

Oddly enough, for surely the most underrated, or at least under-rewarded, player England has ever produced, it could have been so very different if he'd been selected by surely the most overrated, or at least over-rewarded, manager we've ever had. In Euro 96, as England were outclassed and won on penalties against Spain and then outclassed but couldn't apply the killer touch against Germany, you couldn't help wondering how much Matty would have helped.

But for me – first and foremost a Le Tissier fan – it was more than that; on a trip to see the UEFA Cup Winners' Cup final at Wembley, between Royal Antwerp FC and Parma (the latter winning 3-1, I think) I found a copy of *The Mirror*. On the back was a mocked-up picture of Le Tiss in tartan and the headline 'Mac Le Tiss?' suggesting that rejection by Terry Venables meant that Matty was considering playing for Scotland in Euro 96. What truth there was in the story is certainly debatable. In fact it is probably rubbish. Not only had Le Tissier made it quite – and laudably – clear that he was English whoever he might qualify for, but at the time Scotland had not discovered the 'nationality pragmatism' that has served Eire so well since the late 1980s. The Channel Islands were not considered terribly Scottish. On the other hand, the days when Scotland had so much talent that its uncapped players could still have won the European Cup Final twice, were well and truly over (Nottingham Forest's John McGovern). Just as I had felt I might transfer allegiances away from Southampton if Le Tissier left, similarly now I actively considered the plan of becoming the poshest Scot I know (except, of course, for the lot that go to public schools in England or Edinburgh). I drew up mental (by which I mean 'in my mind' rather then the colloquial 'crazy') plans to purchase a dark blue shirt with 'Le Tissier 7' on the back and to see if I could swap my England Euro 96 tickets for Scotland ones.

But just as Matty is said to have told his agent, 'I only want to play for Southampton FC' when Monaco, Internazionale of Milan and even Barcelona were reportedly interested, one cannot really imagine him agreeing to the deal even if Scotland had asked very, very nicely indeed. Matty always made it clear that he was English despite technically qualifying for the home nations and France. He may have been worried by the language barrier. On this occasion I felt his loyalty frustrating; I just wanted to see him on the big stage where he belonged (it could have been for Germany and I wouldn't have cared). Looking back I imagine what might have been. Of course even the slightest changed variable means that for each football match that actually 'happens' infinite other possibilities do not. It is no good transporting another player into the game you lost and saying 'but we'd have won if they'd played' because their presence would have changed all that did happen as well as what did not. But even so, I imagine it is Matty stepping up against Seaman rather then McAllister. And even though at the time – given what actually happened – I was delighted by the save and Gascoigne's second to give England victory, I think I would have got far greater pleasure seeing Le Tissier smash home a gleeful penalty, perhaps later knocking in a trademark volley from distance, only to stand – à la Dennis Law for City against Man U – reflecting on the enormity of what he'd done as the tartan army (with me – and perhaps Dennis – in their midst) went crazy.

But of course that didn't happen. One suspects that 1995/96 did represent something of a decline for Le Tissier because during 1993/94 and 1994/95 Matty had done everything to show that he deserved promotion to the next level. Maintaining that level of performance week in week out when the promotion never really came must have been difficult to say the least, but it was still Le Tissier who saved the Saints. Crucially, he had guided Southampton through that early stage of the Premiership including the year of 4 relegated teams. If, and it is still a big if, Saints now establish themselves as a team that people think big enough for the Premiership, it will be because of Le Tissier's efforts during these years. Even if they do not, Le Tissier ensured Southampton were a top-flight team for longer than anyone might realistically have imagined.

From the following season Le Tiss's brilliance was more sporadic (although surely once again meriting selection for France 98) and players like Berkovic, Ostenstad, Pahars and Beattie finally ensured that the creative and goalscoring duties could be genuinely shared. But in the mid-1990s Le Tissier was absolutely, unquestionably the best; a better example of a *successful* one-man team would be hard to find.

Do They Mean Matt?

Everyone who has liked football has had an opinion on Matt Le Tiss and they all thought they were right. A player rarely seems to have divided opinion as much. Here is a collection of the worship, wonder, irrationality and ignorance. As an experiment, when I started work on this book, I decided to ask friends and friends of friends (most of them not Saints fans) what they thought of him. One of the first replies I got was so vitriolic, however, it took me rather by surprise, finishing with the challenge 'stick that in your book'. OK, I will, but the sender will remain nameless, mainly because I know the unimaginative little t***** nicked it from some Man U fan on a website anyway. It said (with spelling corrected): "... is that the fat unambitious bloke who always flattered to deceive, had a f**kwit of a brother that nearly cost us a place at the World Cup and married the ugly bird off *Home and Away?...*"

Well whether you are the original author of those words, or the bloke who thought it worth plagiarising, I think it is worth pointing out a few things. For a start, let's think about 'unambitious'. First, this seems to rely on defining ambition in a particular way which encourages the idea that greed and glory are automatically to be encouraged, and which equates Manchester United with 'good'. Second it seems to blame Le Tissier for his brother; perhaps those words' author's own Oedipal fantasies mean that he would *actually* like 'to be to blame' for his own brother, but it's not usually a legitimate complaint. And third, at least he's had a bird or two, no he didn't marry her and was she really that ugly? But leaving aside such idiocy, even the more measured responses show a remarkable variation of opinion, even though few seriously dispute the claim of the usually idiotic, but on this occasion spot on, Matt Davies (aka Daphne) that 'Matthew Le Tissier has scored some of the most fantastic goals I have ever seen.'

'If being "lazy" is producing strings of glorious touches, timely passes to team-mates and goals galore, then Robson could do with a few idlers in Italy this summer. Le Tissier might not make it this time but surely in the long run he will not be added to the list of great players

England managers have not had the guts to select.' – sad but true! From The *Southampton Daily Echo*, 25 January 1990.

'You cannot tell me that this man isn't a class act, of huge international quality' – Barry Davies. (I wouldn't dream of it, Barry. Matty had just won a game at St James' Park with a left-foot volley.)

'I don't coach him, it's more man-management. I've just championed his cause.' – Alan Ball, *The Daily Telegraph*, 20 February 1995.

'I don't know why he wasn't taken to France – at least he can take penalties.' Exactly Alan. Alan Ball again in *The Guardian*, August 1998.

'Le Tissier is the most talented footballer in Britain.' Graeme Souness on taking over at Southampton in 1996.

'He's a different class altogether. There's just something about him...he's just got the ability to stroll around and stroke the ball wherever he wants. He should be in the England team and it should be built around him.' One of the not famous ones out of Oasis (Paul) in 1995.

'A couple of years back, Le Tissier spent a season being the greatest genius ever to kick a ball.' Simon Barnes, *The Guardian*, 1996.

'[The banner bore]...a simple message "Brazil would pick Le Tiss" And you know what? They just might' – John Sadler, 1996 after England (minus Le Tiss) lost 1-3 versus Brazil at Wembley in a Euro 1996 warm-up.

'Time for England to play with flair instead of fear. There must be a place for Matt' Headline, *Nottingham Evening Post* after the same match.

'Hey, I'm a mate of Matt Le Tiss, I've got no reason to support England.' Mike Osman gets short shrift from some Scots for wishing them luck in Euro 96, but responds with this, which summed up the feeling of many of us at the time. Amazingly Matt managed not to feel resentful himself.

'It's still Le Tiss or nothing.' Nottingham Evening Post preview of Notts Forest v Saints, 1996. (I just put Notts cos it irritates 'em. They're all so fickle anyway! Most of you can't even remember the '2 European Cups' (Yawn). Come On You 'Pies!)

'Successive managers of the national team overlooked his creative genius in favour of donkeys and hod-carriers many of whom...were not fit to lace his boots.' Well said! Comedian Mike Osman makes a serious point in the Testimonial Magazine.

'Some people may have criticised his fitness, but Tiss does do weights every day – you try carrying 14 stone around!' 'Comedian' John Beresford in the Testimonial Magazine.

'What I have learned to appreciate most about Le Tiss is his ability to still put a smile on my face thinking about the many goals he scored and great games he played. It is always refreshing going through everyday life and then having these happy flashbacks. I loved and will never forget the match against Newcastle when he was under

tremendous pressure to perform and scored those two superb goals. It is the greatest match I have ever attended (closely followed by the England B match against Russia). As a German I am happy he didn't play much for England and never took a penalty! I guess that you can love many things about the man (like putting the ball on Monkou's head when it mattered, making Dowie look good, the way he ambled or his attempts at tackling for instance) but most important was that every match he played in had that promise of a truly special moment. I'm just grateful that he decided to stay with Saints all those years.'
Random German, Herr Karsten Hubscher, Co-Founder of the Bremen Saints. Hoch Die Internationale Solidaritat!

Chapter 5:

Frustration and More Frustration

Under Graeme Souness, Le Tissier started to struggle more with injuries and the weight started to creep on. The new manager clearly didn't value Matty as Bally and Merrington had and though he was still an asset in the Premiership and still knocking on the England door, the late 1990s was a period of several increasingly frustrating seasons. Although Le Tissier is relatively generous about Souness's managerial talents, after being the big fish in the small pond for so long, the same players who under Alan Ball had just got the ball to Matty and then shared the credit (and win bonuses) now failed to stand up for him in a team meeting where Souness pointed the 'does he do enough for the team?' finger. There were still a few great goals left in Matty, but it was the beginning of an end, which new managers tended to contribute to rather than alleviate.

Under Dave Jones, Le Tissier started to struggle more with injuries and the weight started to creep on. The new manager clearly didn't value Matty as Bally and Merrington had. Under Glenn Hoddle, Le Tissier started to struggle more with injuries and weight started to creep on. The new manager clearly didn't value Matty as Bally and Merrington had. At the same time, it must be said, other players began to turn Saints more into a proper team and the new stadium finally happened. Both these factors meant that Saints' Premiership survival now seemed not to depend entirely on the ambling genius from Guernsey. But of course none of this would have happened without said genius, and even during this period of relative decline, his skills still delighted the fans, many of whom would have repaid his loyalty with applause if he'd chosen to play the game drinking pints of lager from a deck chair in the centre-circle.

Thanks

I would just like to say thank you, Matty. It doesn't matter how much we now look like a team, all the Saints fans I know recognise quite clearly the causal link. If there had been no Le Tissier we would be

Bradford, QPR or even Notts County (no disrespect, but they'd probably quite like to be where Saints are now and good though he was, a player only as good as Les Ferdinand could never be good enough to be a one-man team). If not for Matty we would not have a new stadium. We would not have got to a Cup Final or have played in Europe (however brief the Bucharest/Black Sea sojourn turned out). Matty may not have been able to join in these things as a player, but we *know* that without him it would never have happened. We also know that 'nothing good lasts forever' – and we may yet be Bradford, QPR or even Notts County – but then again 'sometimes nothing starts' (The Undertones – 'Julie Ocean').

Despite his amazing contribution prior to Souness, some commentators still seemed determined to persist with the myths they had learned about Le Tiss from his earliest days. Thus, the amazing trickery, the constant delivery of telling crosses and the astonishing pass-completion rate – not to mention the fact that he was often not so much man-marked as man-mugged by 2 or 3 players – Le Tiss never seemed to 'do enough' for pundits such as Alan Hansen. Dario Gradi may have put his finger on the dilemma for some managers when suggesting that you weren't always sure you wanted him in your team, but you were absolutely certain you didn't want him playing for the opposition. At times the opposition spent a lot of time trying to neutralise what was clearly Saints' only significant threat; if despite this he still scored the winning goal or threaded the only telling pass of the match, did this mean he hadn't done enough or ought to contribute more? If as players tired and allowed more space he was consistently at this point able to take advantage, should that have been considered a problem?

Anyway, whilst Motty had his quiet orgasms, Gubba his noisy ones and whilst both and others battled to express their delight and amazement at Saints' 'sorcerer in chief' some, like Hansen – and Martin Tyler – remained determined sceptics. I remain convinced that this has to do with football being a team game; if Matty had been able to cross to himself, run onto his own through balls and so on things might have been very different. But whilst Le Tissier was being a one-man team, so often his team were on the back foot and so often his flicks and through balls went not to clinical strikers and goal poachers but to, well, bless him though he tried, Neil Shipperley. (I have nothing against Neil and I'm glad he's had a successful career. He scored some important goals for Saints and on his Southampton debut mis-kicked home one of 4 great chances to earn a draw in the FA Cup against Luton. But as Trent FM in Nottingham reported a goal he scored for Wimbledon against Forest I cannot help but recall their words of disappointment – 'Aghhh...when he was here [playing for Forest] he couldn't hit a cow's arse with a banjo.' And he'd probably admit he never *really* made it at the top level.)

Back to Le Tissier and 1996/97. Remember this was still a couple of seasons before realistic England claims receded and a season in which he scored the winning goal at St James' Park by being quicker than defenders. As Barry Davies put it, 'don't tell me this man isn't a class act ... of *huge* international quality.' But even so, in the season's opener (0-0) v Chelsea in which Le Tissier hit the bar with an exquisite chip, Martin Tyler suggested that Matty had 'so much to prove after last season's poor output.' It seems Le Tissier had started to be judged against his own standards; thus a season in which he scored a mere 20% of Saints' goals but laid on almost another 60% becomes one of 'poor output'. Perhaps a small, and surely inevitable, dip around the time of preparations for Euro 96 is the reason for such comments? Regrettably one must conclude that not only Tyler but the England manager had failed to notice that Le Tissier was performing miracles with the footballing equivalent of 5 loaves and 2 fishes (you might even say 1 fish, as Ian Dowie had left by then).

It is difficult to be precise about reasons, but however much the pundits may have over-stressed 1995/96 as decline simply because Matty wasn't volleying in from 30 yards *every* week, then 1996/97 *was* different. Perhaps Matty was affected by the negative criticism, perhaps the weight was edging on, perhaps he was disillusioned by not being selected for England? But since he continued to score amazing goals and not move away from The Dell, perhaps not. More likely what changed in 1996/97 was that Eyal 'if ever a player should have stayed at Southampton' Berkovic looked like he might provide a telling pass for a goal and Egil Ostenstad looked like he might score one. And they did. Saints finally looked like they could win without their talisman. And they did. During this season, even discounting games when Le Tiss was injured, suspended or not selected, he 'only' scored or laid on a little under 50% of their goals; perhaps a reason why they nearly got relegated (although that also happened when he was at his best) but more likely the welcome long-term news that Saints were not simply a one-man team any more.

I might be wrong – I often am – but 1996/97 seems to be the beginning of a negative, reinforcing, downward spiral. Le Tissier had always claimed that he got fit by playing; training, practice and bloody-minded determination seemed like short suits in his pack compared to the more laudable pursuits of junk food, beer and women. (As a Liverpool-supporting friend put it, he appeared to be from another planet – albeit a planet where you got to lie in bed for doing good things). He has not hidden his like for junk food, distaste for salad and merely 'theoretical' adherence to the idea that footballers shouldn't drink. But whilst this might be fine for the younger player or 1970s player, later in a career residual fitness declines and proper training/rest regimes – not *just* playing – become essential to prolonged fitness. (As Carter the Unstoppable Sex Machine once observantly put it, 'you wake up one day, you're 24/25 and you think, "my God, I'm a fat bastard."') Along with this, diet becomes more important. Extra weight can lead to extra strain on the body and more injuries and in turn less training/playing. Perhaps. Certainly Le Tissier – at first slowly and imperceptibly and still brilliantly – seemed to decline. And to put things in perspective, his non-inclusion in the 1998 World Cup squad still seems to have been not because he wouldn't visit a personal trainer or dietician and more due to his unwillingness to use a faith healer. In fact faith in his own ability was never required.

And that faith continued to squeeze magic moments out of a declining career and made the idea that he would ever drop down a division unthinkable. 1996/97 was the season of Southampton's 6-3 win over Manchester United including Matty's delicate lob over Schmeichel. (Note to Alan Parry: The 6-3 game and the grey shirt-changing game which we won 3-1 the season before were *not* the same game, OK?!) It is also the season of 'might have beens' internationally. Le Tissier made his competitive England debut away to Moldova, coolly clearing from the edge of his own penalty area but with only 10 minutes to play, when a comfortable England were going through the motions. After then, ignoring him for a couple of games, Hoddle picked him again for a proper start in a proper game against Italy in a World Cup qualifier. Surely it cannot be true that Hoddle was breakfasting with David Icke when his rice crispies started talking to him and said that Eileen said he should pick Le Tiss? In any case, he was in.

Some nice flicks, some blocked shots and a header which went just past the post. If the keeper had stayed on his line and dived it would have looked great; alas as it was it looked a bit like he'd missed an open goal and Le Tissier was lined up as the scapegoat. When he was substituted after an hour, one senses that Hoddle was ensuring that he didn't get to share the 'scapegoatage' that was around. Correctly, but irritatingly, Hoddle later admitted that he shouldn't have taken Le Tissier off, although that doesn't mean he gave him another chance, nor that he ever gave him an explanation for watching him perform brilliantly the following year against Russia B and still not giving him a chance. If Hoddle's behaviour seems like that of a callous lunatic then enough is probably known about Hoddle for me to make no further comment. What might have happened if the header had gone in or one of the crisply struck shots had not been blocked? Small margins indeed!

'Where was Le Tissier?!' I screamed it half a dozen times or so after the defeat to Argentina, in drunken manic despair. We had lost on penalties again and left the world's greatest ever penalty-taker at home. It is easy to think, as Matty scored less than a dozen goals in his post-France 1998 career that Hoddle must have been right to leave him out. It is easy to think, when you see his frame filling out on Sky appearances, that he wasn't in good enough shape. But that's nonsense, and if you reject all other arguments, might not Le Tissier have been a great player to have on the bench when you needed a goal from nothing? The Russia B game was hastily arranged to try out a few players. For Matty it was like saying, 'here it is, the last chance of your career. You've got to take it.' And with all that pressure he pulled off one of the most awesome displays ever. And he still didn't get picked!

One senses that something died in Matty after that. Haven't we all been there? Shall we go to the gym or pop to the pub? And for most of us, safe in the knowledge that we'll never trouble the international selectors, we go to the pub. For Matty that moment was not just a self-serving mock justification but a moment of cruel realisation. How to get motivated after that? But actually, to a certain extent, he did, laying on one and scoring the other as Saints made perhaps their greatest ever relegation escape in 1998/99, taking more than 10,000 supporters to an away game at Wimbledon. At the beginning of that season, with Dave Jones seeming to hint that Le Tissier was surplus to requirements, fans broke into the club's training ground and daubed 'Matty Must Stay' in 6-foot-high letters on the pitch. At the end of the season, although Pahars scored the goals, he was still highly influential in the final-day win against Everton. In between he was still able to shine, nominated *The Sun*'s star man in March's 1-0 win against West Ham, summed up in the elegantly parsimonious phrase 'different class' although they could have just said 'f***ing brill!'

And even after the arrival of Hoddle signalled the effective end of his Saints career, he still managed to return for the last game of 2000/01 and score the last ever goal at The Dell, under Stuart Gray. And he did play in the new stadium although, it must be said, ineffectually. In the final league game of his contract, he got to sit on the bench, although injured and by then clearly not the best option. A nice touch by wee Gordon, although even then the sending-off of Tahar El Khalej meant that tactically it wasn't possible to put Matty on. Disappointing perhaps, but I think most people were relieved not to see how far off the pace he had become; relieved that he did not pick up a further injury which might have prevented him playing in his own testimonial.

And so he did get the sell-out testimonial he deserved in May 2002, with two brothers playing, one refereeing and all Saints fans thinking exactly the same thing as a 10-year-old *Mitchell* Le Tissier banged in 5 goals with either foot including a penalty from the real penalty spot (after Ian Wright had patronised the young lad by putting the ball 6 yards out).

The Penalty King?

This book may raise various arguments which not everyone can agree with. Many people will argue, for instance, despite being completely wrong, that Matthew Le Tissier is not the most special player ever. However, if we move to the spot-kick there can be few such disagreements about who is the best ever; the undisputed penalty king is, of course, me, Lloyd Pettiford. I have now taken around 20 in official fixtures and school matches and 5-a-sides – being only an occasional player – and have never missed. This has included some high-pressure situations including the school bully threatening to kill me if I did miss, and a match-winning penalty against Stoke City for North Staffs Polytechnic in a 5-a-side exhibition. On a trip to Costa Rica in

1993 I even blagged my way into the national stadium for a training session (freelancing for *World Soccer* and they never did bloody publish the stuff) and challenged the bloke who had kept Scotland at bay in the World Cup; slacks and deck shoes were no obstacle as I put it straight in the top corner and he didn't even move, except for raising his eyebrow – perhaps he thought I was Scottish? Enihoo ... back of the net!

Of course others have pushed Matty's claim for the penalty king title. Certainly, despite my deadly accuracy from the spot, my inability to go beyond playing for a school (that hardly ever won) in terms of representative honours, has ensured that my claim is not a high-profile one. In order then to settle the argument once and for all I wrote to SFC at the end of 1995 asking if my wife and I could get married on The Dell pitch and whether they could organise a half-time penalty challenge – me versus Matty. A letter full of rejection soon returned. Still The Dell's loss was Devizes Registry Office's gain. As for the challenge, it was declined too. Of course, I don't really stand by the note in my diary which simply said 'Matty Chicken.' I'm sure he had to listen to team talks or something at half-time (although I did issue the challenge to coincide with a suspension), but I hope the publication of this book will cause him to seek to set the record straight. What a moment to see us both waddle onto the St Mary's pitch! The unspoken nobility of our conflict ... err, etc.

But in claiming my title, it is not just my 100% (get that Matt, 100%, not 98.08%) record that I am appealing to. What is more, and of course by putting this in writing I doom it to become untrue, I am also a penalty good-luck charm, having never seen my team miss a penalty live in a 'career' spanning nearly 1000 games (Bishop's Stortford, Southampton and England).

The only England penalty shoot-out I was at was against Spain in Euro 1996; regrettably for England a tricky situation including a bag of sugar and Zoe Ball had seen me give up my ticket for the semi-final against Germany. When Jim Magilton missed for Saints against West Ham I was in Bolivia. When I first supported Bishop's Stortford, Joey Simmonds never missed, including the FA Trophy semi-final of 1981; and when Duncan Hardy took over duties and completely mis-kicked against Windsor and Eton the goalkeeper had made such a spectacularly early dive that he couldn't get back up to prevent it trickling across the line. In fact I now recall I did see just one miss but it doesn't count. It was the East Anglian Cup Final of around 1985, played at the ground of BSFC opponents Wisbech. This being the most excitement in Wisbech since 1885, the local population – proverbial Adam's apples the size of, well, big apples (and that was just the women) – was out in force; the local constabulary however was not. As Martyn Taylor missed the first, almost quite literally 'sudden death' penalty to hand the match to Wisbech we were all mightily relieved to have been saved a beating from a bunch of mutant yokels with webbed-feet and 11 digits – so I don't really count that as a miss, and more of a blessing! And of course a few years later, who can forget the compensation of the 7-6 penalty win in the Loctite Cup Final … who *was* it against?

Let's say Harrow, although I remember little except a plastic shark and being hungover before I got home.

But seriously, my claim to be penalty king is probably no more preposterous than other claims that have been made and which pale in comparison with MLT. Players who have not missed for a single club, for instance, such as Charlie Mitten, who scored a mere 18 and never missed for Manchester United (but who missed elsewhere). Or players who have taken a lot in one season such as Francis Lee, who notched 15 in one season but nonetheless managed zero from two for England. But none of these claims can be taken seriously – apart perhaps from mine – when compared to the overall record of Matthew Le Tissier. It depends on which competitions you actually include, but Matty took around 50 and missed just once. Not only that, but he hardly ever even looked close to missing. One hit the post and went in and another went in at the angle of post and bar, but mostly they just went straight in the corner and with such power that even when the keeper got a hand to them it was impossible to keep them out. He never resorted to 'straight down the middle' (he claims he didn't have the bottle for that!) so it is not as if the keepers had to think about much.

In fact, possibly the only other person who could even think about being given the title 'penalty king', and for completely opposite reasons, was Bert Trautmann, the remarkable German who marched to Russia in World War 2 and saw most of his mates killed, turned around and marched back to France and saw most of the rest of his mates killed. After that he got captured by the Americans. Then he escaped, and got re-captured by the British. He finally ended up in England where he ultimately stayed, and even more ultimately won over the 'Sieg Heil' and 'Nazi' taunters. Trautmann saved around 60% of the kicks he faced. Now that would have been some contest – Le Tissier against Trautmann. But in the real world, Mark Crossley – the only goalie to save a Le Tissier penalty – also let in the most too. And the only goalie who seemed to have got the measure of him was Ian Walker, but although he got his hand to 3 in consecutive Saints v Spurs matches in 1994/95, he couldn't prevent any of them trickling in the corner.

So what was the secret? In some ways Matty's answers are the same as ever – crediting natural talent as the most normal thing in the world. I guess if you've got natural talent it is the most normal thing in the world. Pick your corner. Keep an eye on the keeper but not the keeper's eyes. Have naturally big thighs (don't bother to train them up or anything) so you can get power and control. Be calm. Have bottle. Think of the crowd. Don't miss an opportunity to score. At the time of writing it seems whatever Matty had, has rubbed off on subsequent Saints penalty-takers, all of whom have reasonable records (Dodd, Magilton, Pahars, Beattie and even Crouch in the 93rd minute to beat Pompey!). Although no doubt putting that in writing will doom it too. But at the moment (famous last words) there are times when it seems the Saints could afford to miss a penalty. But given the one-nil wins and the margin of relegation escapes, not only was Matty a one-man team, but perhaps this single aspect of his remarkable game actually made the difference in itself. Whatever, let's not have any very silly debates about who was the best penalty-taker ever. And apart from creativity, what was England's major failing as a national team in the 1990s?

Chapter 6:

The Greatest Ever Goals in England's Top Division

There has been some conjecture recently as to the best ever goals in the English top division and at least one list was most unsatisfactory in that it didn't even include Matty's personal favourite in the top ten! Furthermore, Dennis Bergkamp's rather fortunate strike against Newcastle *was* in the top ten even though on ITV's highly respected *Premiership Today* programme it wasn't even rated as goal of the day; no that honour went to 'Chris Marsden football genius' for his mazy run from the wing à la John Barnes in the Maracanã against Brazil, the only real difference being that John Barnes had to score against Brazilian so-called 'defenders' whereas CMFG had to contend with the uncompromising toughness and resoluteness of Ipswich Town. As if that wasn't enough, Dalian Atkinson's mazy run and chip was in the top ten although Kevin Davies' more powerful run from the halfway line against Everton was not.

If you are detecting a slight Southampton bias in the interpretation offered here I can only suggest that this is an important corrective to the tendency to regard anything done by Arsenal and Man Utd (formerly Liverpool and now also Chelsea) as better simply because it is done by them; I mean everyone knows that Wayne Bridge (at Southampton) was a better player than Ashley Cole, only enhancing his reputation with superb goal celebrations against Pompey (don't worry, they're unlikely to read *this* book as a reminder of the main reason we were better than them throughout the 1990s). In any case, below I offer my version of English football's greatest goals including a more accurate representation of Le Tissier's own contribution. Before going onto those goals, I should say that you might argue that this section is something of a filler. My initial belief that Matty would be interviewed for the book led me to think of a series of cunning questions to finish the book off with the transcript of an interview. Sources now tell me he *may* simply have been too lazy to contact me! However, questions like 'If Terry Venables had said he'd pick you every game for England if you were playing for Man U, what would you have done?' are too terrifying to contemplate, and questions like 'if you had been guaranteed an

England place could you have eaten salad for 10 years and trained twice a day?' I probably know the answer to already, it being 'no'. As for asking what was going on with the 'cat-fight' at Coventry, I can live without knowing that one. 'Did you ever think about getting a trademark goal celebration?' were rejected early on as too boring. 'Do you want keema or garlic nan with that Jalfrezi?' would have been a nice one to have the opportunity for but that's life. So, on balance, it is possibly better that I now have this chance to put Le Tissier's goal contribution in proper context.

Bubbling Under

Before looking at the top ten itself, it must be admitted that some great goals are not getting in. A couple of great chips by Le Tissier himself, for instance; one of two against Manchester United, for further instance, in a 4-1 win. That game of early November 1986 was reported on by Clive White in *The Times* (November 5 1986, Wednesday) under the headline 'United's Nightmare Returns', with, as ever, reporters concentrating on the fact that the big team conceded 4 rather than that the underdogs scored that number. Le Tissier features only late in the report with a description of 'a curious brace of goals from the young Southampton substitute, Le Tissier, who entered the fray with just 16 minutes remaining. That one of his goals seemed suspiciously offside was of little consequence'; I have watched the video and it is not offside. But presumably the vague possibility that Man Utd might have been victim to yet another outrageous decision against them (it must be 3 or 4 a decade) is more important than describing a super cool finish from a lad barely 18 years old. Makes yer blood boil, eh?

And then there was the 'hat-trick completer' against Norwich City, for example, with an excellently eulogising commentary that I put on my answer-phone; 'please leave a message after the goal'. That's not to mention a stunning swerver against Coventry (although they inevitably equalised in the 106th minute!), the delicate half-volley against Swindon, the rocket against Newcastle (timed at something like 99.6 mph) and the one that had even The Anfield Kop clapping in admiration. A superb goal against Lincoln City to avoid an embarrassing cup exit is also usually forgotten, regrettably and probably because it was against Lincoln.

But apart from these strikes from Le Tissier himself, others are not getting in either. Di Canio's strike which won the competition above really wasn't *that* good at all; 9 times out of ten he couldn't have done it which means there is an element of luck. The Le Tissier strike – which came second – was, by comparison, total control and ease; no luck, just skill. It should have been number one in *that* poll, although, as we shall see, it again misses out here! Was Matty really 'OK' about coming second to Di Canio as he said when interviewed for that programme? He did respond with a typically generous and 'I don't really care' attitude, but I get the feeling he knew the truth.

Amongst others not getting in is Dennis Bergkamp. That one against Newcastle was just too fortunate even if he did intend it and the one against Leicester ... well it wasn't *that* good, was it? Possibly the best goal I saw Dennis score was against Southampton, but that's not getting in either on principle. Still, even discounting the above, there are still plenty to choose from in the countdown of English football's best. You may not agree with my assessment, but if you've enjoyed the rest of the book, you probably will.

English Football's Top Ten Goals EVER

Number 10: *Matthew Le Tissier (Southampton) v Newcastle United (St James' Park), 22 January 1994 (Premier League)*

Well, it is a book about Le Tissier so we may as well start with one of his, although this one must feel unfortunate to be only at number 10. Despite being simply a dead-ball strike, there were many special things about this goal. For a start it came very late on in the game (83 minutes) with the score at 1-1 and won the game for the Saints. Away wins at St James' Park are rare things indeed although Le Tissier was to produce one again a few years later when Barry Davies described him as of huge international class; that left-foot thrash doesn't make it here either, but worth mentioning along with a right-foot thrash which equalised late in the day at The Dell; Tony Gubba described that one as goal of the season in his initial report.

As well as the goal's lateness it also took place at a St James' Park which was being redeveloped meaning that no away fans were admitted. As Sue Mott's report put it, 'Southampton entered a lion's den and did the mauling themselves.' Saints were only still in the game because of a bit of luck and a Le Tissier corner flighted onto the head of Neil Maddison in the fifth minute. In other words this really was a victory against the odds in front of an intimidating crowd. Furthermore the goalie, Mike Hooper, had already been beaten earlier in the season by two wonder strikes in the game when Branfoot had recalled Le Tissier; so Hooper ought really to have known what was coming. Since then Ian Branfoot's unhappy time had come to an end and Alan Ball's almost limitless faith in Le Tissier had seen the Saints turn things around and Le Tissier's form improve out of sight. Even so, this victory was crucial.

So much for the context – which is much of why this goal

was so special – but what about the goal itself? Another one-man special; a long run by Le Tissier himself ended in a foul and gave the Saints a free-kick out on the left with just a bit more of an angle and distance than might be considered ideal. And there's not really much more to be said apart from the fact that Le Tissier just whalloped it and punched the air in eerie silence as the ball whizzed into the top corner of the net. Hooper didn't move and St James' Park just watched in a stunned silence as Matty, pursued by team-mates, ran over to Alan Ball and the bench. 'Alan Ball must have fought to quell hysteria as his new team gloriously grabbed a late winner,' read the report. A good start indeed to our top ten.

Number 9: *Matthew Le Tissier (Southampton) v Aston Villa (Villa Park), 24 August 1994 (Premier League)*

OK, it might be a bit cheeky to include another Le Tissier one so soon, but after keeping the Saints up single-handedly the season before, things had once again started off slowly and a defeat without scoring was the last thing I needed as my Mini Metro moved sluggishly up the A34 en route to Nottingham. However, time *was* ticking away and Saints looked to be slumping to another defeat (1-0) in front of just a few Saints fans midweek at Villa Park. It is probably worth including this one if only to correct the view that all

Le Tissier's great goals came at The Dell (a view only reinforced by descriptions of the wonder strike v Blackburn – Matty's personal favourite – being described and graphically depicted by a popular sport magazine as having taken place at The Dell when it was, in fact, at Ewood Park).

On this occasion, the ball came to Le Tissier, wide-ish right. It didn't look like much was on and time was almost up. However, a casual swing of the boot and the ball went up, curved away and dipped over the goalkeeper into the far corner. It looks so easy that you wonder why everybody doesn't do it every time they are in that position. Of course the answer is that it's not that easy. Against Villa better was yet to come (see later in this list), but Southampton's season had finally got started. Le Tissier just stood and got jumped on by his team-mates – often a preferred technique of his for celebrating at the end of another typically arduous 90 minutes.

Number 8: *David Beckham (Manchester United) v Wimbledon (Selhurst Park), From The Halfway Line (Premier League)*

Many people consider this to be a fine goal; achieving what Pele didn't and accelerating Beckham's catapult to superstardom. But actually, now I think about it, was it that good? OK, he kicked it a long way but the goalkeeper was positioned appallingly and all Premiership footballers should be able to kick the ball the length of the pitch if given that amount of time and space. Roy of the Rovers once scored a goal like this playing in the States (NASL) and the commentator said, 'An opportunist strike there by Roy Race, but oh so boring.' Exactly! So I just stuck this in to give it a bit of realism in case a casual punter walked into Smiths and started flicking through. The real number 8 is described below, but I've had to call it number 7 so that it follows on. The real number 7 will also then have to be called number 7. A bit confusing, I know, but I think we can justify this as 7 is a very special number. Do you follow me?

Number 7: *Matthew Le Tissier (Southampton) v Nottingham Forest (The Dell), 24 March 1993 (Premier League)*

Worth mentioning this game as the one where Le Tissier missed his only penalty (at least for the first team), although he more than made up for it with a sublime strike with his weaker left foot which would have deserved to be the winner of any game but turned out simply to be a consolation in a 1-2 defeat.

A weak defensive header came out to Le Tissier. The possibility certainly existed to bring the ball down and look for an easier shot, but Le Tissier simply lashed the bouncing ball first time into the far corner of the net. I recently showed this goal to some people who had never seen it before and it brought forth audible gasps. Le Tissier also seemed to score many other goals against Forest including an overhead kick at the old Trent End in the days before the Premier League and in the highly prestigious Zenith Data Systems Cup Final (again a consolation). It has to be said though, that unlike Newcastle, against whom Le Tissier also scored frequently, Forest usually came out on top, including a 3-4 win at The Dell in which Matty scored a hat-trick from dead-ball situations. So number 8 and better than Beckham from the halfway line is a scorching left-foot, first-time volley into the top-left-hand corner – is it any wonder no one else gets a look in if that is number 8?

Number 7: *Matthew Le Tissier (Southampton) v Wimbledon (The Dell), 26 February 1994 (Premier League)*

(This is the real number 7. That one above is number 8 if you're confused. The number 8 above that isn't really number 8. If you're confused, go back and read it in order.) On boxing day of this same year – against the same team – I watched Le Tissier mis-control a ball. It didn't happen very often and the Wimbledon fans began to howl in derision. However with the mis-control taking the ball away from him, Le Tissier pounced in an instant and directed a vicious half-volley back across goal. It travelled straight towards me. The keeper had no chance as it flew into the corner of the net right in front of me. Another fantastic goal which looks rather average in the Le Tissier collection. The howls of derision were as still-born as ever cries of derision were. And why Wimbledon fans of all fans would be howling with derision I don't know after what happened on 26 February earlier that year.

On that date Wimbledon fans watched their very negative team emerge pointless from The Dell. Rather than blame their own very negative team they seemed to blame Le Tissier. Le Tissier had been effectively double- and triple-marked out of the game but you cannot mark someone at a free-kick. With the free-kick right on the edge of the 'D' Le Tissier had the ball rolled back to him (by Jim Magilton, I think) and flicked it up and volleyed it in the corner of the net (not in off the post as some reports said – I really do wonder if journos actually watch the games at all). Apparently he had done it 4 out of 6 times in training but almost forgot about doing it in the match. The Wimbledon keeper (Hans Segers, I believe) had previously suggested that Le Tissier was capable of doing this kind of stuff only in televised matches. Wimbledon fans bemoaned that he hadn't done anything else all game. That may be true, but for all the other players on the pitch one might also say that they did nothing all game. As one reporter put it: 'The scorer, predictably, was Matthew Le Tissier, who flicked up and volleyed a free-kick from almost 30 yards with the ease of a man picking cherries. The rest of the game was bilge.' (*The Times*, 28 Feb 1994)

The various headlines of the game probably summed it up between them. In *The People* (27 Feb 1994) Mike Donovan decided that a game with one of the greatest goals ever deserved the headline 'We Were Cheated! Joe Kinnear Furious At Defeat Against Southampton' – quality journalism. The basis of Kinnear's anger was that he sent out Dean Blackwell to mark Le Tissier out of the game; when a free-kick was awarded against him for a bit of holding that does often go unpunished (but is nonetheless against the rules) and Le Tissier scored from the free-kick, that counts as being cheated! So *The Sunday Times* and Vince Wright probably get much closer to the mark with 'Le Tissier Delivers Moment Of Magic' (27 Feb 1994) and Michael Henderson in *The Times* (28 Feb 1994) is spot on with 'Kinnear's Bluster A Sideshow To Striker's Brilliance'.

Just for the record it seems Kinnear really lost the plot that day, defending those mid-90s Wimbledon angels in the face of appalling refereeing! One of his complaints, amazingly, was that refs are 'trying to take the law into their own hands'. As Michael Henderson noted at the time: 'The rotten bounders! Any day now policemen will try to apprehend robbers.'

Number 6: *Matthew Le Tissier (Southampton) v Manchester United (The Dell) When We Beat Them 6-3 and Roy 'Can You Really Believe He Is Supposed To Be One Of The Best 100 Footballers Ever? No, Neither Can I' Keane Got Sent Off, No Doubt For One Of Those 'Uncharacteristic' Bits Of Violence That Seem To Have Afflicted His Game*

Am I mistaken, or are goals like this normally given much more coverage? This one seems almost to have been overlooked. Indeed I was thinking of omitting it myself until I realised that any opportunity to mention Saints beating Manchester United 6-3 ought to be gleefully taken. Perhaps the excellence of a Berkovic volley and a hat-trick for Ostenstad meant it got lost? (Even though the FA Premiership Panel of Meanies eventually took away Egil's third goal.)

But anyway, while the score was 0-0 (and the celebratory atmosphere of later still a long, long way away) Le Tissier – on the edge of the box – twisted a bit this way and a bit that way and then casually chipped the ball up and over one of the best goalkeepers supposedly ever to have played in this country. Absolutely fantastic but perhaps, and understandably, overshadowed by the result and possibly

Ferguson dominating all post-match analysis with talk of grass-length, injury time, shirt colour and any other possible excuse as to why his team kept getting thrashed at The Dell by relegation-fodder!

As a footnote, Peter Schmeichel – who is almost as irritating to listen to as his name is difficult to spell – was recently asked (commenting upon Spurs 4-5 Arsenal) if he'd ever been involved in a 9-goal thriller. Amazingly, he came up with the answer, 'yes, twice,' mentioning just an 8-1 win at Forest and a 9-0 crushing of Ipswich. Well I think we have to put on record that Peter was also in goal on this glorious day!

Number 5: *Matthew Le Tissier (Southampton) v Arsenal (The Dell), Last Ever Goal At The Dell (Premier League)*

Another left-foot volley and a fitting end to an emotional day at The Dell. Saints fans knew by this stage that Matty would never be the same player, but they also knew in the final 10 minutes on The Dell pitch he had a chance to do something and they had a chance to say thank you very much indeed. Both happened in an extraordinary finale to a great stadium and, many would argue, the greatest player ever to play there.

After appeals for a penalty were turned down, correctly, it

seemed like Le Tissier might not score the 'inevitable' winner against the League Champions (I think they were, though I care not). However, he popped up in the box, swivelled and volleyed past understudy to one of the greatest goalies etc. If I sound a bit vague in my description it's because I was sitting on a wall outside The Dell with a view somewhat obscured by other walls and jolly miffed to see Jean Tigana leave a few seconds before and not even give me his ticket. By the time I saw the goal on *Match of the Day* I had been celebrating for several hours and curiously I've not had the chance to see it much since.

The newspaper take was this. 'Matt Signs Off With A Sizzler' said Steve Young in *The Sunday Express* (20 May 2001) saying of the last goal in a 3-2 win that 'Fittingly, it was Le Tissier who had the final say. He seized on a loose ball 12 yards out and pivoted to curl his shot beyond Manninger and into the top corner.' Steve also pondered on what Le Tissier might manage if he could get fit! Elsewhere, Roy Collins of the *Sunday Telegraph* was considerably more realistic, starting his report by suggesting that 'Matt Le Tissier is almost as much a relic as the condemned Dell these days' before going on to describe the wonderful goal and rightly pointing out that despite increased girth and injury 'he never lost his place in the heart of the club's supporters, grateful for the many times his spectacular goals rescued them from relegation in years gone by.' And in *The Sunday Times* (20 May 2001) Brian Glanville ('Le Tissier Has The Final Word') summed the whole thing up: 'Romance in football is not quite dead. For there could scarcely have been a more romantic ending to Southampton's 103 years at The Dell. Eighty-nine minutes had gone when Matt Le Tissier, so long the idol of the crowd, brought on as a substitute, spun on the ball to strike a glorious left-footed shot past Alex Manninger to win Southampton a game they had seemed likely to lose.'

Number 4: *Matthew Le Tissier (Southampton) v Liverpool (The Dell), 14 February 1994 (Premier League)*

Side-footing with great power, Le Tissier didn't always give the impression of hitting the ball very hard. However, he could and did. In this example, and a last-minute equaliser v Newcastle which doesn't make this list but which was one of the fastest shots ever at around 100mph, Le Tissier proves that he can hit shots more blistering than anyone. This one was in the St Valentine's Day massacre of Liverpool, 4-2 and they were lucky to get the 2.

The game had only just kicked off when the ball arrived on the edge of the box and Le Tissier just thrashed it first time. It hit the back of the net without bouncing – beating Grobelaar at his near post – and without ever getting more than 18 inches off the ground. As ever the purists will be disappointed with Le Tissier's overall contribution. Despite scoring a hat-trick and taking the corner from which Saints' other goal was scored, he did have an opportunity to make it 5-0 which was brilliantly tipped round, and at no point appeared to be running around like a headless chicken or Robbie Savage.

This goal was a choker for the away support. Many, without tickets, had been trying to harangue the mostly overseas students of Southampton University with flats in the very descriptively named Overdell Court. Those who got in were doing what all away teams did at The Dell before someone finally realised that *we* would be better off with *them* in a corner; namely starting the game in tremendous voice aided by the compact and acoustically amplifying Archer's Road End. Liverpool, Liverpool they sang. The strike was so swift and 'out of nothing' that some didn't have time to stop singing before they were trailing 1-0. When Craig Maskell later scored from a Le Tiss corner they must have known it wasn't their night!

Number 3: *Matthew Le Tissier (Southampton) v Blackburn Rovers (Ewood Park), 10 October 1995 (Premier League)*

Oh dear! Once again Matty's personal favourite fails to be regarded as the best goal ever, even by one of his loopiest fans. I'm not sure what it is? Perhaps it is that Tim Flowers is so comprehensively beaten that he seems unable to get himself anywhere near the ball; as if in some way it *must* be a goalkeeping error? Or perhaps it is simply that by this stage you really were *expecting* him to score. After all, in this match he had already scored a half-volley from the edge of the penalty area which for many players would have been the pinnacle of a goal-scoring career. So when he ambles and swerves around the centre circle and looks to be shooting from fully 35 years, where else is the ball likely to go?

Of course it went in the back of the net, and as at Anfield in a goal a bit like the number 2 goal below but not quite as good, the home fans graciously applauded. Since Liverpool won 4-2 and Blackburn 3-2 that might have something to do with the grace of the applause, but even so this was something special. Once again, a goalie made the mistake of taunting Le Tissier, claiming that a goal scored the previous week – perhaps by Alan Shearer – would win goal of the season. It didn't. This did.

As Martin Searby put it in *The Sunday Times*, 'Le Tissier Turns On Magic But Rovers Prevail'. He might have added the word 'sadly', once again Le Tissier's best meaning a slightly worse goal-difference when it could have won international football matches, even if Southampton 'were unfortunate to leave Ewood Park with nothing to show for their contribution to a competitive game illuminated by the marvellous Le Tissier.' And I must have pointed out earlier in the book how Le Tissier's figures were better than Shearer's when they played together? Searby is astute enough to recognize that that remained the case even as Shearer played for a top side up front and Le Tissier in midfield for strugglers (both took penalties, it's just Shearer sometimes misses): 'His two strikes quite overshadowed another brace for Shearer, who, with his partner Sutton, accounts for more than 70% of Blackburn's goals. Last season, Le Tissier's 25 were one more than the rest of his side could muster between them; now he has 14 of 30 in all competitions, a figure which compares favourably with Shearer's 19 out of 41.' I like this Searby fella! He goes on: 'Le Tissier gave them the jitters every time he touched the ball and one turn and deliciously weighted pass was better than anything Rovers managed.' Why did no one listen to him: 'Never mind the inconsistency; players with his ability must be part of any national team aspiring to success on the world stage.'

Number 2: *Matthew Le Tissier (Southampton) v Newcastle United (The Dell), 24 October 1993 (Premier League)*

Le Tissier scored twice in this game. One was in the 86th minute and won Southampton the game. As with so many others I keep remembering, like the juggle against Liverpool which got applauded by The Kop, it should really be in a list like this in its own right, but in this game it was overshadowed by the goal that came second (somehow) to Paolo Di Canio in Sky TV's Premiership Top Ten. So, how does Matty come second again here, with a goal I have already described in such eulogistic terms elsewhere in the book? All will be revealed, but I can assure any of you who are worried that he is not beaten by Di Canio on this occasion!

No, in fact the only thing spoiling the aesthetic beauty of the goal was a knock down by Ian Dowie immediately prior to it. In order to bring it under control, Le Tissier had to flick it up and over his head with the outside of his left boot. Then, as Barry Venison rushed towards the ball, Le Tissier managed to keep it close enough to flick it over him and then up and over/inside Kevin Scott. With the goalie – the hapless Hooper – to beat, Le Tissier calmly slotted the ball home, later claiming modestly that he slightly mis-hit it.

Number 1: *David Beckham (Engerland) v Greece (Old Trafford), 2002 World Cup Qualifier*

Don't panic! Of course this isn't the real number 1. However the point of putting it here, apart from once again wrong-footing the casual browser, is to make an unfortunate point about all those goals that Matty scored. Yes, we had a few in the last minute. Yes, we had some 1-0 wins. Particularly we saw some high-pressure penalties 10 minutes from time. Lots of goals that kept Saints up, but it is rather sad (perhaps fitting in the context of his particular career) that there was never that truly great moment – like Beckham against Greece – when you felt that all your Christmases had come at once. The Newcastle goal – above – was something like that, but not quite. Thus despite the exquisite beauty and power of Le Tissier's goals we were still left wanting 'that' moment. For a long time I assumed that it would arrive in a World Cup final, especially that of 1998; I assumed that sometime, sooner or later, justice would be done in terms of the whole world knowing what I knew; that we had here the most special of special talents. But it never did and the almost limitless sense of possibility was destroyed by the passage of time.

(But anyway, before moving on, Beckham's Greece goal wasn't *that* good. The George Clooney lookalike didn't even jump, let alone dive!)

Number 1 Really!: *Matthew Le Tissier (Southampton) v Aston Villa (The Dell), 19 December 1994 (Premier League)*

But that's why my favourite Premiership and Le Tissier goal was scored against Aston Villa. Unlike most of the above I was not actually there, as I may have mentioned earlier, as we were at the beginning of those now regular – but still irritating – Sky schedule changes. So I watched this game getting drunk in the pub. It is a game Villa probably deserved to win. And it was a free-kick that Southampton probably didn't deserve to be awarded and one which should very likely have been saved in any case. But the intensity of alcoholic intoxication, the holiday atmosphere and the ever-present reality that 3 points rather than 1 might be what would keep Southampton up at the season's end were what most closely recreated in this goal the type of moment experienced when a late goal secures World Cup qualification, a League Championship (like I'd know!) or victory in an FA Cup final.

This free-kick looked too far out, to be honest, and the shot, accurate and side-footed, looked like the sort that might earn a corner but not a goal; and a corner was normally the minimum we would expect in these situations. To be honest I thought the kick would waste enough time to secure the point. But then again, Le Tissier's side-foots were deceptive and this one was simply palmed into the corner of the net. The match was won, the commentators wanted to change their man of the match. Le Tissier just stood as if to say 'I told you so'.

I have never celebrated a goal so much and it's my book, so that was the best goal of all time. Oh yes. Thank you.

Conclusion:

They Were God Times Indeed

The Le Tissier story may seem like a sad one. Certainly from a fan's perspective I look back on it as a Brighton fan must look back at the 'Smith must score' moment in the 1983 Cup Final; moments from Matty's career just get replayed over and over in my mind. The half-volley as substitute on his debut for England v Denmark (well struck but over the bar). The right-foot control and left-foot volley v Romania (well struck and just over the bar – enough to worry the keeper). The header v Italy and the blocked shots seemingly arrowing to the corners. The unusually poor free-kick in what few minutes of the Eire game were played.

But I have already mentioned these moments and I should not torture myself, or you, with their repetition. Smith's miss *would* have won the Cup Final, but any of these things might have changed nothing. A perfect performance versus Russia B changed nothing. It was the stubborn insistence of England managers in settling for mediocrity rather than gambling on glory, and their refusal to give the best player in the country a run in the team which are to blame.

And don't be fooled – if, as many suspect, the pounds creep on with each Sky appearance – into thinking he was *just* another good player; look back to TV coverage from that era (*Match of the Day*'s man of the year for 1994, for instance) and newspaper or other interviews and absolutely everyone – including even Graeme Souness and Glenn Hoddle – regarded Le Tissier as *the* best player in the country. Brazilian friends of mine in particular could not work out the logic of his absence from the England team. However, Le Tissier himself seems irrepressibly happy. His friends and fans still spit feathers (though I've never been sure what that phrase really means, mind you) at the Venables era and then Russia B, but he himself seems genuinely to follow the 'my way' doctrine and to realise actually just how lucky in life he's actually been.

Though this book has concentrated on a 'what might have been' playing career, from the point of view of today Le Tissier doesn't look to have much to grumble about. He's now played regularly for the England team, albeit at beach soccer, looks quite quick (or at least not very terribly slow) as one of the youngest 'Masters' players and got his first proper adult honours as former Saints' colleague David Hughes's team Eastleigh won the Jewson, Screwfix, Wessex (something?) League. He's on the TV a lot, 'muppeting' for Sky almost as extravagantly as he played and, quite rightly, played for the 'Legends' in Sky's bizarre celebrity/reality TV show *The Game*. He also swans around the new stadium being cheered/worshipped and plays golf and caddies. Marylin's been replaced (Sallyanne), but presumably whoever partners Le God will have their own opinion on whether 90 minutes of lethargic love-making followed by a few seconds of ecstasy really makes it worth all the lying back and thinking of England ... or at least England B.

Le Tissier's appearance in the Southern Masters Tournament of 2003 allowed his fans another glimpse of the great man, but in some ways it was a depressing parody of his entire career. The tournament is for over-35s. Le Tissier was not playing because his body looked old enough, but because you have to be over 35 at the end of the tournament year – he was 34 and would be. Oddly enough though, it looked like this might be one of his last Masters tournaments, despite his barely qualifying on this occasion.

Never one to be described as gaunt myself, I nevertheless have to say that Le Tissier easily looked the heaviest and least fit player on show. When you think of the players of his skill who have gone on playing for much longer and until much older it is, in a way, a crying shame...but then I'm trying to keep this conclusion cheerful.

And in fact, it was just like his career where appearances were often deceptive. Within seconds of starting the opening game against Chelsea the barrel-chested deity (well, 'barrel-bodied' actually) had played a 1-2 with Francis Benali, feinted sublimely and then dragged a shot in at the far post to open the scoring. Moments later and a clever piece of trickery saw a volley come back off the post. Soon after that, however, he needed a breather and sent on Craig Maskell as substitute, even though the rules help by requiring one player at all times to remain in the opposition's half (now imagine how good Le Tiss would have been if 'goal-hanging' were a real position!?). Back for the second half and Le Tissier forced a brilliant save before Michael Gilkes got a Southampton second – from a Le Tiss assist of course. Then 'our hero' – who had created the lead – gave the ball away a couple of times and Chelsea came back to draw 2-2. Just like the old days but in an old men's kick about and with no irritating pundit claiming he didn't track back enough.

In the next game against Fulham they got wise to him and responded as many teams tried over the years by 3 men surrounding him each time he got the ball. This actually created so much space that Le Tiss was able to play in Francis Benali to score. Matty then scored a penalty. He then tried a nutmeg ... it worked, but he was just too slow to get around the other side and grabbed the player to pull him back. David Elleray – who never gave Saints much anyway – gave a free-kick against him. It was just like the old days. (Although a Franny Benali volley meant a 4-3 win to Southampton, so not exactly like the old days.) Against Portsmouth Matty rested himself at the start, perhaps anticipating the punch-up, and then popped on to put in Cockerill with an audacious flick. Then he missed an open goal and Benali overtook him in the scoring. At that point, like at the end of his career, you could sense it was all going wrong.

Pompey Goal

Rumours abound of Steve Claridge's testimonial and Le Tissier appearing in a Pompey shirt, scoring a penalty and taking off his 'Portsmouth' shirt to reveal a Saints one emblazoned with the word 'scummer'. Did it happen? Matty scoring for Pompey ... makes you shudder! However, I have seen the photographs even though I have vowed never to suffer the pathetic vitriol of Fratton Park again.

By the time of the final, Le Tiss wasn't fit enough to play having picked up a back injury. I suspect – having suffered similarly – that backs do not take kindly to carrying all that weight around. He did come on, however, and gave the ball away as Chelsea scored their second on the break. Again he gave the ball away, tricking a player with his brain and feet but without the freedom of movement to get round him. He claimed, as he had to the nice Mr Elleray, that it was a foul but it really just looked like his frustration; he can still do the tricks but can't catch up with his own flicks. Chelsea scored their 4th and Le Tissier was sent off. Matt, interviewed by Sky TV, seemed as convinced of injustice as ever – 'the ref doesn't know what he's doing' – but it was truly a sad end, although I dare say he'll appear in another beach soccer game or on a 5-a-side court sometime. This book doesn't pretend to be autobiography-like in its scope, but it is good to see that Matty still looks happy and relaxed, and that the pounds haven't (yet) piled on as they might.

So, was MLT a genius who scored some f****** great goals, had a f****** big nose and who blew it all (not the nose), *not* in some frenzy of booze, drugs and a wild rock'n'roll lifestyle but apparently – and maybe even more tragically perhaps – on kebabs and a genuine ability not to be really very much arsed whether anyone else thought he was the best because *he* knew he was the best and was having a very nice life thank you very much?

Burger

Former Saint Richard Hall said that he welcomed the chance to be a part of Matt's testimonial committee in order 'not only to recognise the part he has played in Southampton Football Club's history, but also to hail a man who can demolish three quarter-pounders with cheese, large fries and a large coke in one sitting.' (Testimonial Magazine)

Booze and Birds

In answer to the question 'So you can only drink a very limited amount when you're playing?' in his testimonial magazine, Matty says, 'I don't know about that – in theory, yes.' In the same magazine John Beresford advises Matt, 'Don't go chatting up any birds where there's a boyfriend with a bottle in his hand!' and Alan Mullally says, 'Over the past year I have had my fair share of nights out with Le God (drinking of course!).'

Although some people may wish to suggest it is so frustrating that Matty did not make more of himself, others still agree that he was simply the best. We have already discussed the ambition thing – and there are a lot of miserable people who have nonetheless managed to 'make the best' of themselves of whom we might ask 'what was the point?' Le Tiss might have easily done everything that was asked of him and still been pilloried in the press. Then again he might have won us the World Cup. It is probably more relevant as a tribute to note that there are a lot of children running around at St Mary's these days who turn around when one father shouts, 'come here Matthew!' What we do in life echoes throughout history, as the saying goes. Who said that? Chief Sitting Bull, was it? Or Larry Grayson? I'm not sure.

For Southampton supporters (and if you are not one, try to imagine that he'd played for you) it was nice (understatement of the decade) to have a genuine world-class player. At the time of writing (and I am writing the conclusion first because the conclusion was always going to be 'he was God') Wayne Bridge has just signed for Chelsea for £7 million. Wayne is a very good player. As a childhood Saints supporter Wayne has also – in my view – missed the chance to be the new Matt Le Tiss. Except, perhaps *that* is the point. Could Wayne Bridge ever have been adored as much as Le Tiss (given that he's *only* very good)? And *would* Wayne Bridge, as a Saints fan, have wanted to be the new Matt Le Tiss? Having played in the losing team in a cup final *and* understudied to a clearly inferior player for

England[6] maybe he has realised that that's exactly what he didn't want?

But the point is – for us, the fans – these are times when the mighty Bishop's Stortford FC (ooh, I do hope that gets past the proofer again) can't resist the allure of Dagenham and Redbridge (despite beating them 1-2 in the 2004/05 FA Trophy 3rd Round). Dagenham and Redbridge (Walthamstow, Leytonstone and Ilford) – in turn – can't hold onto players wanted by, say Oldham, who in turn lose players to Southampton who themselves will lose talent to Chelsea, Arsenal and Man Utd, who might themselves be vulnerable to advances from Real Madrid, Barcelona or Juventus. And it was in *these* days, when we had a world-class player who played and stayed at Southampton despite the world being seemingly determined to identify the reasons he should leave. In their 'cross-over' time at Southampton Shearer and Le Tiss were both highly rated. Shearer, the forward, was out-scored by Le Tissier (the attacking midfielder) in 4 of their 5 seasons together. It may be argued that a move away from The Dell was crucial to Shearer's development and that Shearer's goal-scoring record improved dramatically, but as with so many others, promising talent played out its best years elsewhere. But not so with Matthew Le Tissier.

---

[6] Actually, Ashley's very good. Maybe there's room for them both...?